RAILWAY ATLAS OF IRELAND

THEN & NOW

PAUL SMITH AND KEITH TURNER

Great Southern & Western Railway passenger locomotive No.36 of 1847, built by the Liverpool firm of Bury, Curtis & Kennedy and now preserved at Cork (Kent) station. One of the GSWR's earliest engines, No.36 was withdrawn in 1874 and set aside for preservation and display as a relic at an earlier age. Thanks to some narrow escapes down the years, she has happily survived to this day. *Harry Maeers*

Ian Allan PUBLISHING

THIS BOOK IS DEDICATED
TO
DEBRA AND PATSY KEOGH

OFFICIAL

RAILWAY MAP

OF

IRELAND

PREPARED AND PUBLISHED
AT
THE RAILWAY CLEARING HOUSE
LONDON
1920.

Scale, 1 inch to 7¼ miles = 1/475200
STATUTE MILES
0   5   10   20   30   40

Drawn and engraved by
J. & W. EMSLIE,
LONDON.

The title cartouche on the 1920 Railway Clearing House map of Ireland reproduced in this Atlas.

First published 2014

ISBN 978 0 7110 3796 0

Published by Ian Allan Publishing

an imprint of Ian Allan Publishing Ltd, Hersham, Surrey KT12 4RG.
Printed in Bulgaria.

Visit the Ian Allan Publishing website at www.ianallanpublishing.com

INTRODUCTION

This atlas not only provides, in one volume, a direct comparison between the extensive railway system of Ireland on the first day on 1920 – before a succession of sweeping changes altered it forever – and the stripped-down one of today, but also records the current use made of abandoned lines and closed stations.

The 'Then' maps are faithful reproductions of the relevant sections of the Railway Clearing House's 1920 map of Ireland; the 'Now' maps show all open lines and stations of the current island-wide network (together with any other public railways more than one mile in length) plus a record of all closed lines and stations, especially those now open to the general public in a different guise – be they preserved railways, tramways, roads, cycle trails, shops, museums or whatever.

Out of respect for privacy those stations converted into private residences or commercial premises have not – with a few exceptions – been noted.

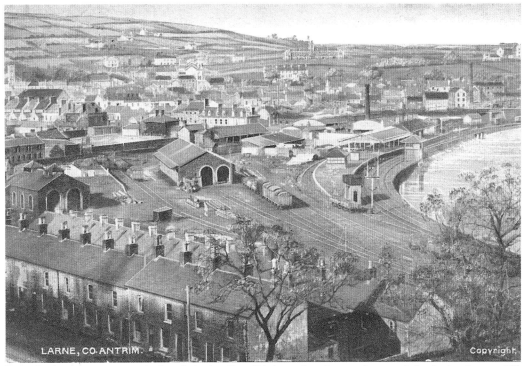

LARNE, CO. ANTRIM.   Copyright.

By far the shortest steamer crossing from Ireland to Great Britain was from Larne to Stranraer in Scotland, a distance of 36 miles. This postcard by Chas L.Reis of Dublin, Belfast and Glasgow, shows the former BNCR Larne Station – with its two engine sheds – on the shore of Larne Lough; the 1-mile extension to the harbour continues off to the right.

The station closed in 1974, replaced by Larne Town a little nearer the harbour, and a slight track deviation made to allow for the construction of a dual-carriageway across the old site.   *K.Turner Collection*

ACKNOWLEDGEMENTS

Special thanks must go to Michael McMahon for casting a knowledgeable eye over the first rough draft of the map pages, and for his invaluable comments and suggestions, and to Paul Jordan for his expert assistance with the preparation of the maps; we should also like to thank Harry Maeers and Jan Dobrzynski for the loan of accompanying photographs and ephemera. Finally, we are indebted to Peter Waller for suggesting the idea of this Atlas in the first place, and to our Editor, Nick Grant, for meticulously seeing it through to completion.

THE RAILWAYS OF IRELAND

While a comprehensive overview of Irish railway history is beyond the scope of this Atlas, it is however hoped that the following notes – together with the potted histories of individual railways and tramways accompanying the maps – will cover and add depth to the most important features.

A SMALL BEGINNING

In their nearly 200-years' lifetime the railways of Ireland have been witness to many changes and innovations, nearly all of which have been paralleled by similar events in Great Britain (and indeed other European countries): from just one or two short lines whole systems have grown, false starts have been made, companies have gone bust or been taken over, networks have been nationalised (and ruthlessly pruned), small-scale electrification has been tried as well as wholesale dieselisation, and preservation schemes have flourished or withered.

The first public railway to open in Ireland, on 17 December 1834, was the 6-mile Dublin & Kingstown Railway built on the route of a horse tramroad in order to improve travel between Dublin and the developing port of Kingstown (now Dun Laoghaire). From that small beginning grew Ireland's Railway Age.

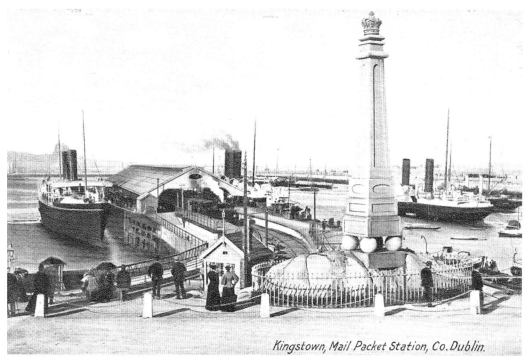

A W.Lawrence of Dublin postcard of the harbour terminal at Kingstown (later Dun Laoghaire) c.1900, with a train just visible in the station. Note the small crowd of interested spectators – some apparently on the railway line!   *K.Turner Collection*

A QUESTION OF GAUGE

Just as in Great Britain, by the 1840s the question of what gauge a new national railway system should have raised itself as it became clear that different railways, sooner or later, might wish to be physically linked. In Great Britain the choice was between George Stephenson's 4ft 8½in and Isambard Kingdom Brunel's 7ft 0¼in – in the event a Royal Commission came down on Stephenson's side. In Ireland, the Dublin & Kingstown had adopted 4ft 8½in whilst the Ulster Railway of 1839 had chosen 6ft 2in; other railways were being planned with possibly other gauges. The Board of Trade therefore stepped in and, taking note of the advice of George and Robert Stephenson to opt for something in the region of 5ft/5ft 6in, came up with the perfect compromise of 5ft 3in for future lines – and for existing ones, of necessity, after regauging.

NARROW GAUGE

As well as having a different standard gauge, Ireland possessed a network of linking, or closely situated, narrow gauge railways unlike anywhere else in the British Isles save the far smaller one on the Isle of Man. Beginning in the 1870s with the two Ballymena lines, these railways served mainly the rural central and western parts of the island beyond the north-east/south-east coastal strip. By 1910, after the opening of the Strabane & Letterkenny Railway, over 550 miles of route had opened, all of 3ft gauge – the same as that adopted in the 1870s as standard gauge on the Isle of Man. This choice by a close neighbour, of a gauge ideally suited to a terrain similar to that of Ireland, must have been a significant factor in Irish promoters' opting for the same; it is also no coincidence that the Isle of Man's locomotive builder of choice, the Manchester firm of Beyer, Peacock & Co, supplied similar engines to the Ballymena & Larne Railway.

LLSR No.10 *Richmond* at Fahan, on a Buncrana-bound train. Built by Kerr, Stuart in 1904, she was not scrapped until 1954 having worked until the demise of this extensive narrow gauge system.   *K.Turner Collection*

LIGHT RAILWAYS AND TRAMWAYS

Another marked feature of the Irish railway scene was the blurring of the distinction between conventional railways (both standard and narrow gauge) and light railways and tramways. Ireland-specific legislation such as the Tramways Act of 1860 (and its 1871 amendment allowing the use of mechanical power), the Tramways & Public Companies (Ireland) Act of 1883 and the 1889 Light Railways (Ireland) Act helped facilitate the construction of cheaply laid and operated roadside lines, especially as rural feeders into towns and cities or to mainline railways. In this way the lengthy and expensive process of obtaining a full Act of Parliament for a line was bypassed; moreover, a system of state grants and guarantees meant that lines were built where they would not otherwise have been, thus increasing their proliferation.

TOURISM

Hand-in-hand with the spread of light railways and tramways (and the more conventional narrow and standard gauge lines) came the development of a new, much needed industry in Ireland: tourism. Now delights such as the Giant's Causeway and the Lakes of Killarney could be sampled by city dwellers on a day's excursion. In addition, holidaymakers could be attracted from across the sea, the British railway companies not being slow to promote their own particular steamer routes from Scotland, England and Wales to the eastern and southern coastal ports of Ireland. Railway-owned grand hotels were built, guidebooks were published extolling the beauties of the Irish landscape and its historic ruins, and the attraction of leisure activities such as fishing, golf and bathing. Scores of postcards were printed by the railway companies to publicise such sights and activities (several of which are included in this atlas) – and, of course, to promote the railways that would take you there.

A Tuck's postcard advertising the former BNCR's grand Northern Counties Hotel at Portrush, inherited by the LMS. The legend on the reverse proclaims that the hotel is in an 'Ideal location facing the Atlantic Ocean: Close to the finest Golf Links in Ireland: Within easy reach of world-famous Giant's Causeway.' *K.Turner Collection*

Converted steam trailer No.7 makes a stop on the Giant's Causeway tramway in early third-rail days, with the majestic ruins of Dunluce Castle as a backdrop. This was a favourite viewing-point for tourists – many of whom have been painted onto a heavily retouched photograph before this Chas L.Reis of Dublin postcard was published! *K.Turner Collection*

AMALGAMATION

During World War I the railways of Ireland, like those of Great Britain, were taken under Government control. This state of affairs lasted until August 1921; four months later a Peace Treaty, coming after decades of political unrest and an increasingly violent insurrection, resulted in the formation on 15 January 1922 of the Irish Free State, or Eire, comprising the whole of Ireland with the exception of the six north-eastern counties of Antrim, Armagh, Down, Fermanagh, Londonderry and Tyrone. To say that this settled matters would be a gross understatement for the next fourteen months saw the new country engulfed in a civil war between the Government and the anti-Treaty faction of the former Irish Republican Army. Railway infrastructure suffered greatly during the conflict and in 1924 the Railway Act provided for all railways wholly within Eire – with the exception of the Listowel & Ballybunion monorail! – to be amalgamated as from 1 January 1925 as the Great Southern Railways.

In the six counties of Northern Ireland – now with its own provincial Government – the railways within, and crossing, the border carried on much as before, the only effect of the similar 1923 Grouping of railways in Great Britain being that the NCC was now part of the London, Midland & Scottish Railway.

NATIONALISATION

As a direct result of the damaging (in so many ways) effects of World War II, the British Government was forced to nationalise almost all public transport in Great Britain, using the Transport Act of 1947 to establish the British Transport Commission; railways were managed by its Railway Executive agent (and 'branded' as British Railways). As for Northern Ireland, the NCC became the Railway Executive, Northern Counties Committee until 1 April 1949 when a new public body, the Ulster Transport Authority, was established to take it over along with other railway and road transport in the province; at the same time the BCDR was bought by the UTA. (See the individual histories for the fate of other railways.) In 1967 the UTA was abolished, with the railways becoming Northern Ireland Railways the following year. Today NIR is a subsidiary of the Northern Transport Holding Company, a public corporation with the brand name of Translink.

Nationalisation in southern Ireland occurred in two stages: on 1 January 1945 a Government-financed company was set up, Coras Iompair Eireann – or Irish Transport Company – responsible for all public transport in the country. This was fully nationalised from 1 June 1950 and since 1986 has been the holding company for Bus Éireann (Irish Bus), Bus Atha Cliath (Dublin Bus) and Iarnrod Eireann (Irish Rail). Together with NIR, IE operates the Dublin-Belfast service.

PRESERVATION AND REUSE

Whilst Ireland can boast its fair share of railway stock and other relics preserved both north and south of the border, in national collections and dedicated society museums, the restoration of derelict lines to an operating condition has lagged far behind similar ventures in Great Britain. The reason for this is simple: the comparative population size and its distribution within the two islands. To buy, rebuild, operate and maintain 10 miles of railway in the one would be much the same as in the other – but with only a fraction of the number of enthusiasts and visitors to support and finance such a project in Ireland, which helps explain why railway preservation projects are moderate in size and few in number compared with their counterparts across the sea, and why several schemes have sadly failed after their initial launch.

Ireland's low population density has however had one benefit: whilst traces of roadside lines have been largely obliterated by road improvements, abandoned trackbeds abound in rural areas as unofficial footpaths – an increasing number of which have been upgraded and given official status as walkways and cycle paths.

CLR No.2 *Kathleen*, a Robert Stephenson & Sons of Newcastle-upon-Tyne 4-4-0 tank engine of 1887, now proudly displayed in the Ulster Folk & Transport Museum Cultra, together with one of the railway's original coaches. *Harry Maeers*

THE RAILWAY CLEARING HOUSE

The Railway Clearing House was a London-based organisation established in 1842 at the behest of the London & Birmingham Railway. Its purpose was to standardise, as far as possible, railway operations in Great Britain (and, by extension, Ireland) and to facilitate through travel of passengers and freight over different companies' lines, with each company receiving a proportionate share of the fare or rate of carriage charged, the accounts being settled by the RCH in accordance with the relevant paperwork submitted by the companies. One of the RCH's most important early decisions was to have its participating companies adopt Greenwich Time, not local time, at all of their stations, and hence in their timetables, while other major agreements came in the standardisation of signalling and telegraphic procedures.

Commencing with just a handful of companies, by 1914 the RCH had nationwide membership. Following the nationalisation of virtually all of the railways in Great Britain in 1948 the role of the RCH gradually diminished, though it was not until 1963 that it ceased to be.

THE RCH MAPS

Of particular relevance to this Atlas is the role played by the RCH in the mapping of British and Irish railways. From 1851 onwards a few RCH employees had, on a semi-official basis by drawing on RCH data, published maps showing the precise locations of different companies' lines, junctions with rival or neighbouring companies' lines, passenger and goods facilities, who had running powers where, and so on. In 1895 this increasingly important adjunct to the business of the RCH was taken over by that body, with sheets thereafter being issued periodically covering the whole of England, Wales, Ireland and Scotland - the last such publication, in 1960, being a map of that country.

THE RCH JUNCTION DIAGRAMS

Like the Maps, the Junction Diagrams – recording precisely where one company's responsibility ended and another's began where two or more different railway's lines physically met – were published on a regular basis, either in loose-leaf or in collected book form (and, like the Maps, checked for accuracy by the companies themselves prior to publication). The example below, published in 1904 for the town of Antrim, shows the nature of the information conveyed.

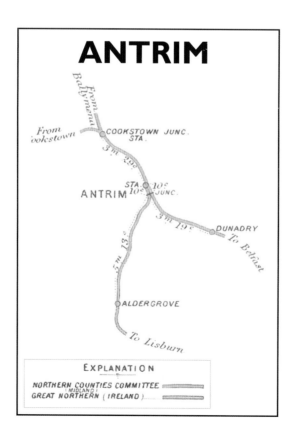

INDEX

Names and abbreviations (where used) of railways, tramways and associated bodies in the text of this Atlas, with numbers of the maps showing the lines and the pages with relevant historical notes.

KEY TO MAP PAGES

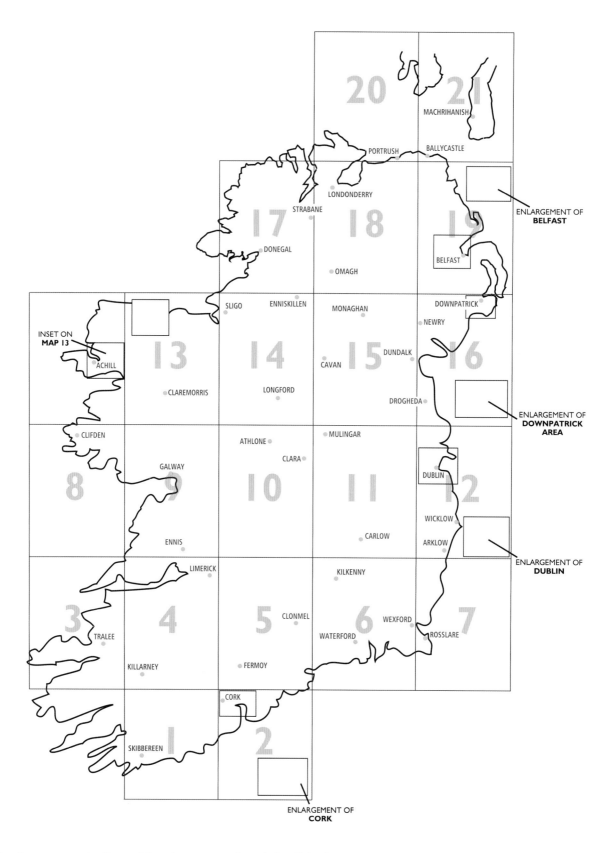

ENLARGEMENT OF
BELFAST

INSET ON
MAP 13

ENLARGEMENT OF
**DOWNPATRICK
AREA**

ENLARGEMENT OF
DUBLIN

ENLARGEMENT OF
CORK

'*Then*' maps are indicated by the numeral and the '*Now*' maps by the numeral followed by the letter A.
'*Then*' and '*Now*' maps are located opposite each other for easy reference

SCALE OF MAPS 1-21 IS **7.5 MILES : 1 INCH**

NOTE - 1 JANUARY 1920 MAPS

These maps are faithful reproductions of all those sections of the 1920 RCH map of Ireland showing railway lines. They have been checked to ensure they depict the state of Irish passenger lines (with some freight-only spurs and extensions marked) as of 1 January 1920; any amendments or supplementary notes deemed necessary have been gathered in the Legend below each map.

Note that the same colour could indicate different railways on different areas of the map, and that no conventional key was included.

JUNCTION DIAGRAMS

These are individual Junction Diagrams, or have been extracted from multiple-place ones, published by the RCH prior to 1920. Each individual Diagram, or page of Diagrams, had its own Explanation by way of a key - again note that the same colour was used for different railways on different pages. (Where one Diagram has been extracted from a multi-place page for use in this Atlas, an appropriate modified Explanation has been created.)

KEY - 1 JANUARY 2014 MAPS

STANDARD GAUGE LINES

Passenger stations and halts open as of 1 January 2014 .... CARLOW

Passenger stations and halts open as of 1 January 1920 but closed as of 1 January 2014 .... DRUMREE

Passenger stations and halts opened post-1 January 1920 but closed as of 1 January 2014 .... HOSPITAL HALT

(Main criterion for inclusion being the existence of a platform)

Freight-only lines ....

Mothballed lines as of 1 January 2014 ....

Lines relaid as tramway systems as of 1 January 2014; only converted stations marked .... DUNDRUM

Preserved/heritage railways with principal stations open as of 1 January 2014 .... DOWNPATRICK

Major railway heritage centres/museums ....

Lines relaid as narrow gauge railways with principal stations as at 1 January 2014 .... KILMEADAN

Trackbeds officially designated as cycle/walkways ....

Trackbeds now roadways N70

NARROW GAUGE LINES & MONORAILS

Lines and stations open as of 1 January 1920 but closed as of 1 January 2014 .... SCHULL

Preserved/heritage railways with principal stations open as of 1 January 2014 .... DROMOD

SHEDS & WORKS

Railway works and principal engine sheds/tramway depots open as of 1 January 1920 ....

Motive Power Depots open as of 1 January 2014 ....

MAP 1

1 JANUARY 1920

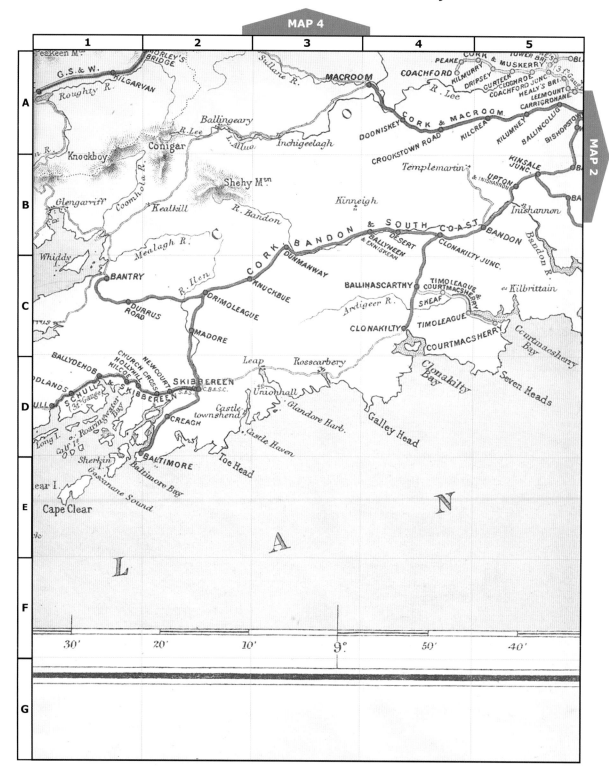

MAP 4

MAP 2

LEGEND

All lines 5ft 3in gauge except:
3ft gauge SCHULL & SKIBBEREEN RAILWAY (D1 – D2)
3ft gauge CORK & MUSKERRY LIGHT RAILWAY (A4 – A5)

A1 KENMARE: Also timetabled as KENMARE FOR PARKNASILLA
A4 CROOKSTOWN ROAD: Originally named CROOKSTOWN & RYECROURT
A5 COACHFORD JUNCTION: Originally named BLARNEY JUNCTION
B4 BALLYNEEN & ENNISKEAN: Correct name was BALLINEEN & ENNISKEAN
B5 KINSALE JUNCTION: Originally named CROSSBARRY
B5 UPTON & INISHANNON: Correct name was UPTON & INNISHANNON. Originally named BRINNY
C2 AUGHAVILLE: A request halt existed 2½ miles east of DURRUS ROAD (See MAP 1A)
C4 BALLINASCARTHY: Originally named BALLINASCARTY. Station shared by the CBSCR and the TCLR

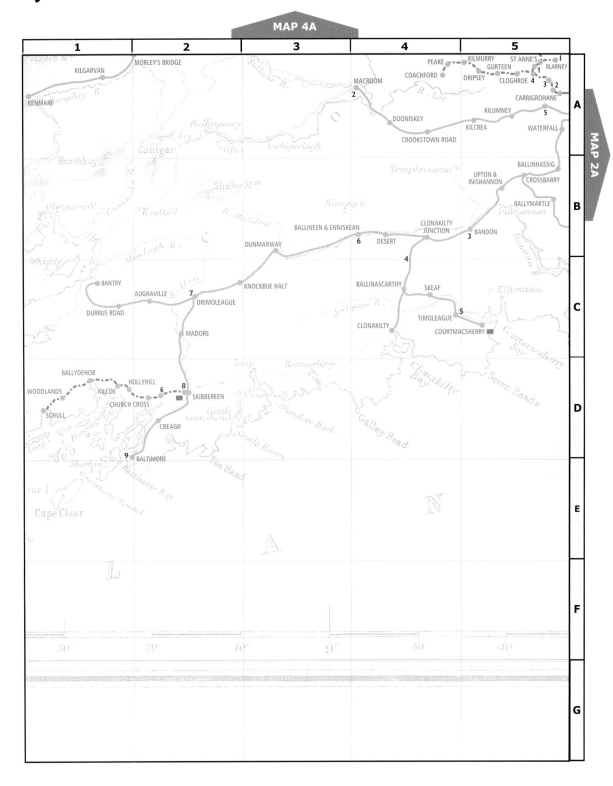

MAP 4A

MAP 2A

LEGEND

1 BLARNEY: Former station building now a gift shop; much of the site cleared as a car park for Blarney Castle
2 MACROOM: Former station buildings now industrial units
3 BANDON: Former station building now used by the county council; former goods shed now a shopping centre
4 BANDON – BALLINSCARTHY: Parts of the trackbed now under realigned sections of the N71
5 TIMOLEAGUE: Site largely cleared as a car park
6 BALLINEEN & ENNISKEAN: Former goods shed now used as a golf club
7 DRIMOLEAGUE: Site largely cleared as a car park, tennis court and a playground
8 SKIBBEREEN: Former station building now part of a garage
9 BALTIMORE: Former station building now home to the Glenans Irish Sailing Club

STATIONS
1. TOWER BRIDGE
2. LEEMOUNT
3. HEALY'S BRIDGE
4. COACHFORD JUNCTION
5. BALLINCOLLIG
6. NEWCOURT

SCHULL & SKIBBEREEN RAILWAY

Officially a tramway, though in reality more of a railway, the Schull & Skibbereen was a 3ft gauge (mainly) roadside line operated by the Schull & Skibbereen Tramway and Light Railway Co Ltd. Some 15½ miles in length, it was authorised by an 1883 Order-in-Council under the provisions of the 1883 Tramways and Public Companies (Ireland) Act to link the two towns of its title (as part of a grander scheme). A short freight-only extension served the harbour at Schull. Opened on 6 September 1886, it became part of the GSR in 1925; the final train ran on 26 January 1947, a casualty of a coal shortage – a legacy of the war years. Official abandonment came in 1952.

SKIBBEREEN STATION

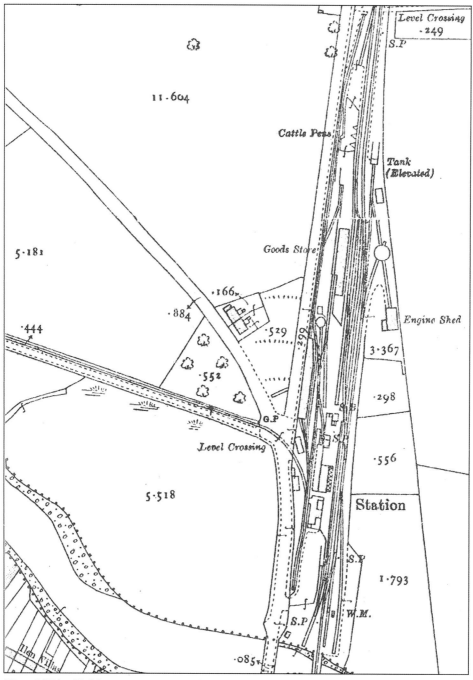

The SSR's Skibbereen station, from the 1941 Ordnance Survey 25in to 1 mile map. The CBSCR's line from Drimoleague to Baltimore runs north-south whilst the narrow gauge line departs westwards along the north side of the Schull road (and in usual Irish fashion, unfenced from it).

SCHULL STATION

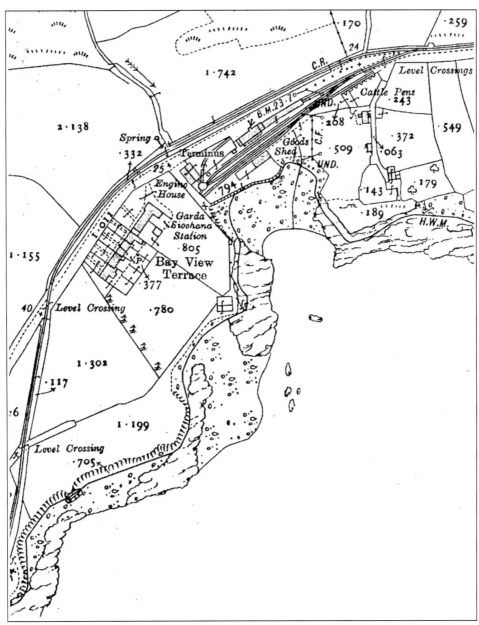

The SSR's Schull station, from the 1941 Ordnance Survey 25in to 1 mile map. The track disappearing bottom left is the goods-only extension to the harbour - a line rejoicing in the grand authorisation title of the Schull & Skibbereen Extension Tramway and Light Railway.

THE TIMOLEAGUE & COURTMACSHERRY LIGHT RAILWAY

The Timoleague & Courtmacsherry Light Railway was a 9-mile single-track branch running eastwards from Ballinascarthy, on the CBSCR's own branch to Clonakilty, to Courtmacsherry on the coast. Nominally the line comprised two light railways, the Ballinascarthy & Timoleague Junction (opened 20 December 1890) and the Timoleague & Courtmacsherry Extension (opened 23 April 1891 as a roadside tramway), worked by three tank engines. The line was taken over by the GSR after the 1925 Amalgamation and closed on 1 June 1925; Government pressure however led to its reopening on 1 September that same year. Regular passenger services ended on 22 February 1947 (though summer excursions from Cork continued); complete closure came on 31 March 1961, the same time as the lines of the former CBSCR.

MAP 2

1 JANUARY 1920

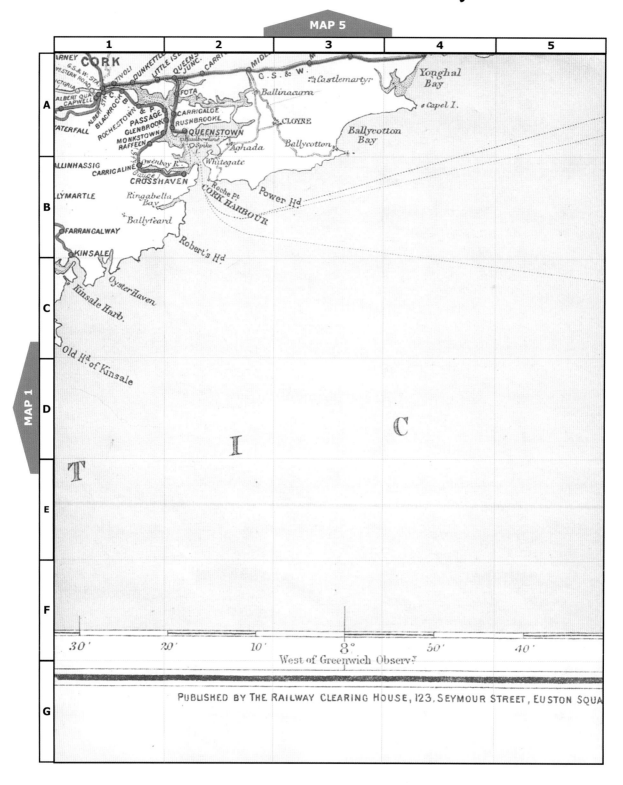

LEGEND

All lines 5ft 3in gauge except:
3ft gauge CORK & MUSKERRY LIGHT RAILWAY (A1)
3ft gauge CORK, BLACKROCK & PASSAGE RAILWAY (A1, B1 – B2)

A1 The five CORK termini were named
    CORK ALBERT QUAY [CBSCR]
    CORK ALBERT STREET [CBPR]
    CORK CAPWELL [CMDR]
    CORK GLANMIRE ROAD [GSWR]
    CORK WESTERN ROAD [CMLR]
A1 RAFFEEN: Also timetabled as RAFFEEN FOR SHANBALLY
A1 SHOW GROUND HALT: An untimetabled halt existed between CORK ALBERT STREET and BLACKROCK,
    used for special events between c1910 and c1932. (See MAP 2A)
A2 CARRIGTWOHILL: Originally named CARRIGTOHILL
A2 FOTA: Originally named FOATY
A2 RUSHBROOK: Originally named MONKSTOWN FERRY
A3 MIDLETON: Originally named MIDLETON, BALLINACURRA & CLOYNE

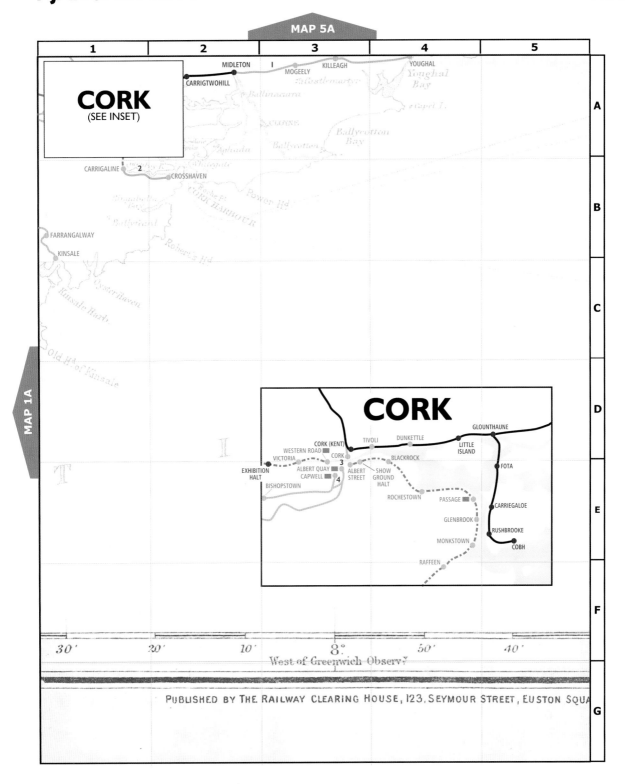

PUBLISHED BY THE RAILWAY CLEARING HOUSE, 123, SEYMOUR STREET, EUSTON SQUA

LEGEND

1 MIDLETON – YOUGHAL: Rails lifted but trackbed reserved for possible reopening
2 CARRIGALINE RAILWAY WALK. www.carrigaline.ie
3 CORK ALBERT QUAY: Now a parking fines office
4 CORK CAPWELL: Now Capwell bus station

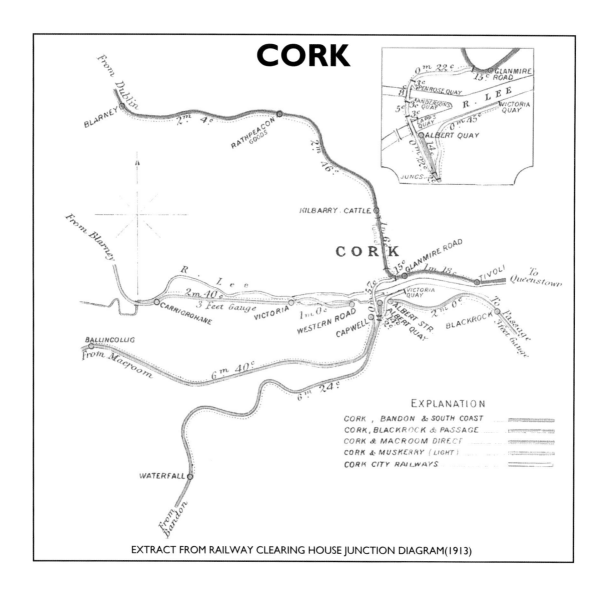

EXTRACT FROM RAILWAY CLEARING HOUSE JUNCTION DIAGRAM(1913)

THE CORK, BLACKROCK & PASSAGE RAILWAY

Incorporated in 1846, the Cork, Blackrock & Passage Railway ran from its own terminal station in Cork southwards to Crosshaven at the southern end of Cork Harbour. The first section of the railway, built to the 5ft 3in gauge, opened on 8 June 1850 and covered the 6½ miles from Cork to Passage. Under the 1896 Cork Blackrock & Passage Extension Act a further 9½ miles of line from Passage on to Crosshaven were opened; this extension was built to the 3ft gauge (to reduce costs, with the original portion of the railway being converted accordingly) and opened in sections between 1902 and 1 June 1904.

The line became part of the GSR in 1925, and was closed in 1932: Crosshaven to Monkstown on 3 May and Monkstown to Cork on 10 September.

THE CORK & MACROOM DIRECT RAILWAY

The Cork & Macroom Direct Railway Company was incorporated on 1 August 1861 to construct and operate a standard gauge line between the places of its title. It opened on 12 May 1866; at the Cork end of the line it joined the CBSCR main line a mile out from the latter company's Albert Quay terminus, which it shared until 27 September 1879 when it opened a ¾-mile extension into its own station at Capwell. Removal of the link to the CBSCR meant that the CMDR became isolated from the rest of Ireland's railways; the link was reinstated in 1918 for military use and upgraded after the railway became part of the GSR in 1925 and on 2 March that year Albert Quay became the terminus for passenger trains over the line once again. These services were withdrawn on 30 June 1935, with final closure coming on 30 November 1953.

The railway employed, over the years, six small tank engines and, briefly (1928-1930), a steam railcar.

THE CORK & MUSKERRY LIGHT RAILWAY

The Cork & Muskerry Light Railway operated a small 3ft gauge system 26½miles in length to the northwest of Cork, with outlying termini at Blarney (opened 8 August 1887), Coachford (18 March 1888) and Donoughmore (6 May 1893); this last branch was owned by the Donoughmore Extension Railway Company but worked by the CMLR. The whole system was absorbed by the GSR from 1925 onwards and closed in its entirety on 29 December 1934.

The railway operated a total of nine tank engines, of which two survived the closure with one going to the SSR and the other to the TDR.

THE CORK, BANDON & SOUTH COAST RAILWAY

The third railway system operating to the west of Cork was the Cork, Bandon & South Coast Railway which, with 104 miles of routes, far exceeded in size the other two combined. Authorized by the Cork & Bandon Railway Act of 21 July 1845, it began in a modest way with the section between Ballinhassig and Bandon opening on 30 July 1849. The system then grew (and absorbed lines promoted by other interests along the way) until it stretched to Bantry (opened 1 July 1881) and Baltimore (opened to passengers 2 May 1893) in the west, and to Kinsale (27 July 1863) and Clonakilty (28 August 1886) on the south coast; the company's change of name came in 1887, to reflect its new extent of operations. Not until 1912 though, with the opening of the CCR link, was the system connected to any other railways (apart from, briefly, the CMDR).

In 1925 the CBSCR became part of the GSR, then in turn the CIE. Apart from the Kinsale branch, which had closed in 1931, the whole system was shut down on 31 March 1961.

THE CORK CITY RAILWAYS

The Cork City Railways Company nominally owned a ¾-mile single-track goods tramway link along the roadway between the CBSCR's Albert Quay terminus (and Victoria Quay) and the GSWR's Glanmire Road station (and Penrose Quay), crossing the twin channels of the River Lee between them by way of lifting road/rail bridges. Incorporated in 1906, the CCR Co was owned jointly (in decreasing size of share) by the GWR (then trying to gain a foothold, by way of its ferry routes from Wales, in the area west of the city), the GSWR, the CBSCR and the Cork Harbour Board.

After its 1912 opening the link only ever saw a regular passenger service for just the summer of 1914 - and by only one return train a day at that. Goods workings ceased in 1961 and in 1980 the river bridges were rebuilt as fixed road structures.

MAP 3

1 JANUARY 1920

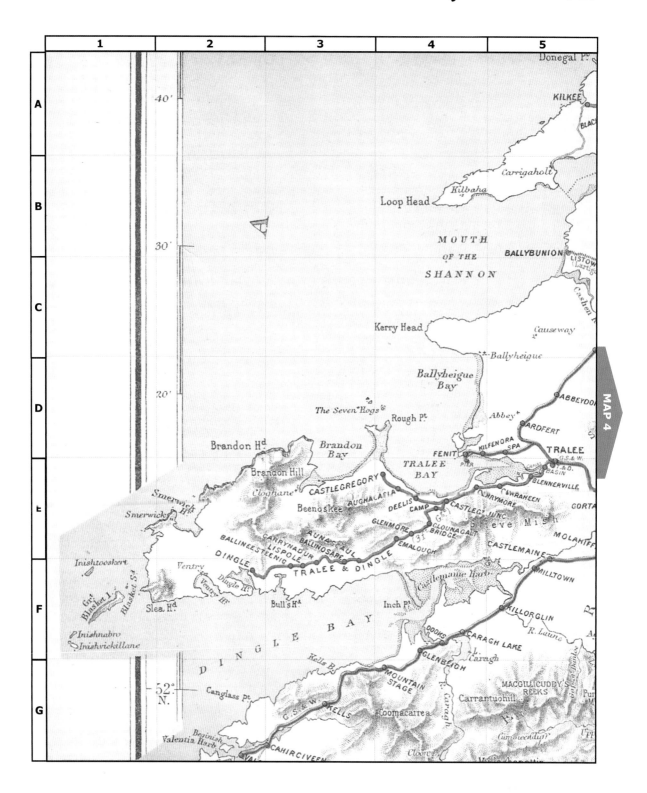

MAP 4

LEGEND

All lines 5ft 3in gauge except:
3ft gauge TRALEE & DINGLE RAILWAY (E5 – F1)
3ft gauge WEST CLARE RAILWAY (A5)
Lartigue monorail LISTOWEL & BALLYBUNION RAILWAY (B5)

FENIT pier line (D4 – E4) freight-only
B5 FRANCIS ROAD: A halt existed here midway between BALLYBUNION and LISELTON (See MAP 3A)
E4 CASTLEGREGORY JUNCTION: Originally named CAMP JUNCTION
F3 BALLINEESTEENIG: Correct name was BALLINASTEENIG
F4 CARAGH LAKE: Full name was CARAGH LAKE FOR GLENCAR
G2 VALENCIA HARBOUR: Also timetabled as VALENTIA HARBOUR

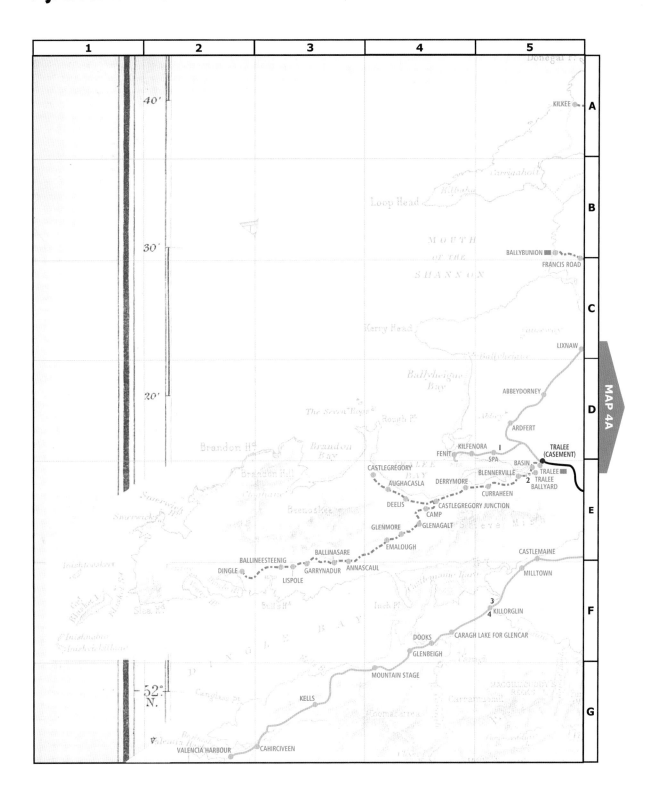

MAP 4A

LEGEND

1 TRALEE – FENIT: Former trackbed being developed as part of the GREAT SOUTHERN TRAIL. www.southerntrail.net
2 TRALEE (BALLYARD) – BLENNERVILLE: Preserved section of the TDLR (operational 1993 – 2006) currently subject of a
   reopening proposal. www.traleesteamrailway.webs.com
3 Killorglin, or Laune, Viaduct immediately east of KILLORGLIN now carries a footpath over the River Laune
4 KILLORGLIN: Former station building now the head offices of a financial services company

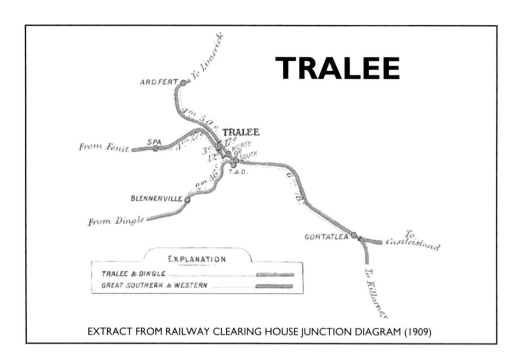

TRALEE

THE LISTOWEL & BALLYBUNION RAILWAY

Perhaps the most fascinating – and certainly the most distinctive – of all the Irish railways was the Listowel & Ballybunion, the only passenger monorail of its kind in the British Isles. Opened on 6 March 1888 and running for just over 9 miles from the GSWR's station at Listowel to the seaside resort village of Ballybunion, in County Kerry, it operated on the Lartigue Elevated Single Rail Railway system, a design invented by a Frenchman of that name. The idea behind the design was to provide a quick and easy means of laying a railway across rough terrain without the need for expensive earthworks, utilising a single running rail mounted on the top of, and a guiding rail each side of, a series of metal A-frames or trestles. The railway's three Hunslet 0-3-0 tank engines each had two boilers hanging down one each side of the running rail, while the carriages and wagons were similarly 'double-sided' so as to balance them on the track. Drawbridge-like structures were provided at the line's 'level crossings'.

The owner of this remarkable line was the Listowel & Ballybunion Railway Company, incorporated by Act of Parliament on 16 April 1886, with operations continuing until, excluded from the Amalgamation, it closed on 14 October 1924, so bringing to an end a unique chapter in Irish – and indeed British – railway history.

THE GREAT SOUTHERN & WESTERN RAILWAY

At the time of the 1925 Amalgamation the Great Southern & Western Railway was by far the largest railway in Ireland, with over 1,100 miles of routes owned or worked, and over 500 locomotives built or acquired by then. Incorporated by Act of Parliament on 6 August 1844, it began in a comparatively modest way with a single line, nearly 56 miles in length from Dublin Kingsbridge to Carlow, opening on 4 August 1846; thereafter it lived up to the promise of its title by spreading further southwards and westwards, absorbing a number of smaller concerns as part of the process until it in turn became (the largest constituent) part of the GSR. Its main lines have survived, and today comprise the bulk of Ireland's railway network.

A Lawrence of Dublin postcard of the Ballybunion terminus of the LBR. Note the Lartigue system's unique 'double-sided' design of locomotive and carriages, and the rotating curved track section able to serve as a point as well as a more conventional turntable. *K.Turner Collection*

Another Lawrence postcard, this time an atmospheric view of a mixed-working about to cross the Cahirciveen Viaduct over the Caher estuary on the GSWR's long route down to Valencia. *K.Turner Collection*

THE TRALEE & DINGLE RAILWAY

The 3ft gauge Tralee & Dingle Railway, incorporated under the Tramways and Public Companies Act 1883, served the sparsely populated Dingle peninsula in County Kerry. Its main line ran from its own station in Tralee (with a short street tramway extension to an exchange siding at the GSWR's station) for 31½ miles to the coastal town of Dingle; this was opened on 31 March 1891, as was a 6-mile branch to Castlegregory. With its long, undulating roadside stretches of track running through a virtually deserted countryside, and with its mixed goods/passenger trains, the TDR was the quintessential Irish narrow gauge railway. Meagre passenger revenues led to the demise of that service on 15 April 1939, though goods workings between Tralee and Dingle (principally for cattle) lasted – barely – until 27 June 1953.

Motive power, over the years, was supplied by nine tank engines of which one (No.5, a Hunslet 2-6-2 of 1892 vintage), after many years retirement in the USA, was shipped back to work the short restored section of the railway outside Tralee – service currently suspended.

MAP 4

1 JANUARY 1920

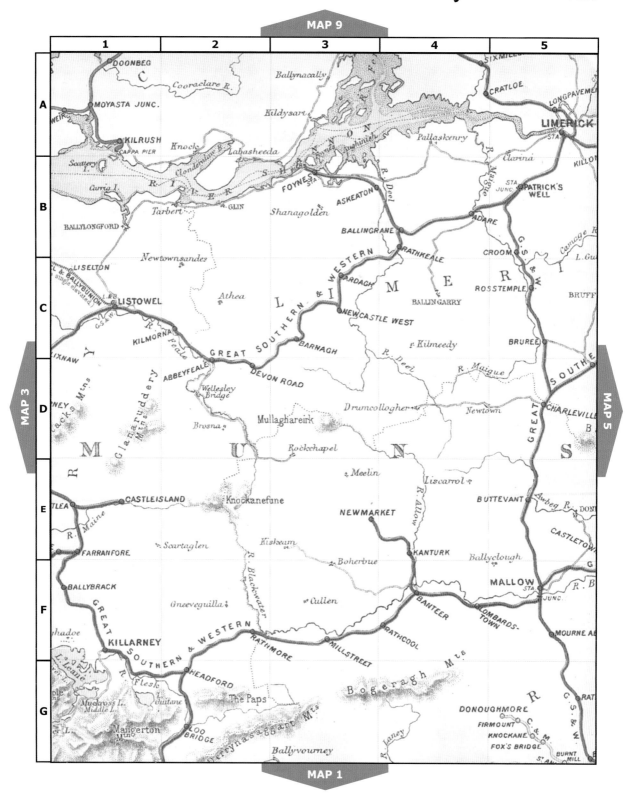

MAP 9

MAP 3

MAP 5

MAP 1

LEGEND

All lines 5ft 3in gauge except:
3ft gauge CORK & MUSKERRY LIGHT RAILWAY (G5)
3ft gauge WEST CLARE RAILWAY (A1)
Lartique monorail LISTOWEL & BALLYBUNION RAILWAY (C1)

A1 CAPPA and pier freight line also used for annual excursion trains
A5 LONGPAVEMENT: Originally named LONGPAVEMENT, the correct name was LONG PAVEMENT
B3 FOYNES: Pier line, freight-only
B4 BALLINGRANE: Originally named RATHKEALE
E2 BUTTEVANT: Full name was BUTTEVANT & DONERAILE
G2 HEADFORD: Correct name was HEADFORD JUNCTION

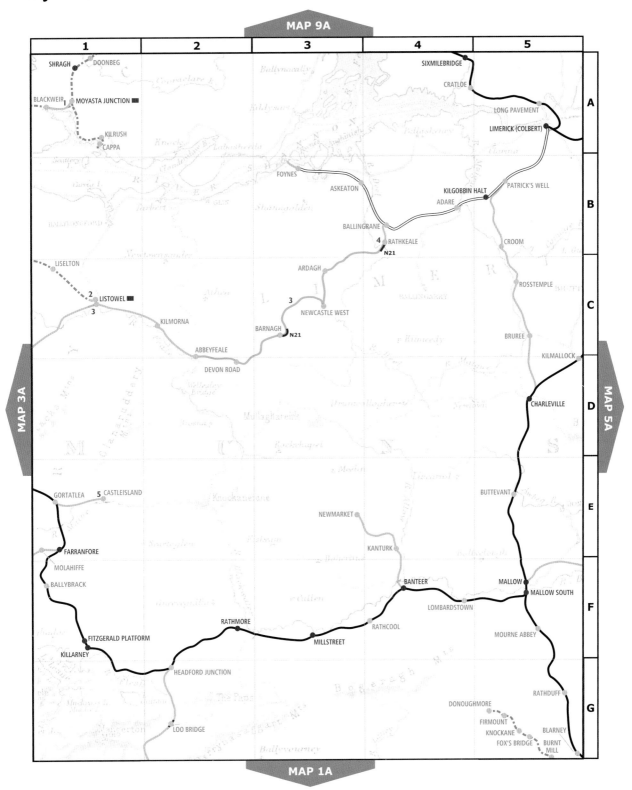

MAP 9A

| | 1 | 2 | 3 | 4 | 5 | |

SHRAGH · DOONBEG
SIXMILEBRIDGE
CRATLOE
BLACKWEIR · MOYASTA JUNCTION
LONG PAVEMENT
KILRUSH
CAPPA
LIMERICK (COLBERT)

A

FOYNES
ASKEATON
KILGOBBIN HALT · PATRICK'S WELL
ADARE
BALLINGRANE

B

4 · RATHKEALE
CROOM
N21
ARDAGH
LISELTON
ROSSTEMPLE

C

2 · LISTOWEL
3
3
NEWCASTLE WEST
KILMORNA
BARNAGH · N21
BRUREE
ABBEYFEALE
KILMALLOCK
DEVON ROAD

D

CHARLEVILLE

MAP 3A

MAP 5A

GORTATLEA · 5 CASTLEISLAND
BUTTEVANT

E

NEWMARKET
FARRANFORE
KANTURK
MOLAHIFFE
BALLYBRACK
BANTEER · MALLOW
MALLOW SOUTH
LOMBARDSTOWN

F

RATHMORE
RATHCOOL
FITZGERALD PLATFORM
MILLSTREET
MOURNE ABBEY
KILLARNEY
HEADFORD JUNCTION
RATHDUFF

G

DONOUGHMORE
FIRMOUNT
BLARNEY
LOO BRIDGE
KNOCKANE
FOX'S BRIDGE · BURNT MILL

MAP 1A

LEGEND

1 3ft gauge WEST CLARE RAILWAY. wwwwestclarerailway.ie
2 LISTOWEL: Former GSWR goods shed now a railway museum, Section of former LBR trackbed
   now home to a diesel-powered replica monorail. www.latiguemonorail.com
3 Part of the GREAT SOUTHERN TRAIL, www.southerntrail.net
4 RATHKEALE: Former station building now the Irish Palatine Museum and Heritage Centre.
   www.irishpalatines.org
5 CASTLEISLAND: Site cleared as a supermarket car park

An LNWR official postcard advertising the 'Royal Mail Route' from Holyhead to Dublin, then on (as the legend on the reverse proclaims) 'to Killarney, Cork, Waterford and the South and West of Ireland'.

K.Turner Collection

Five more LNWR official postcards featuring its own (and one other) Irish Sea vessels, beginning with the 1897 twin-screw steamer *Cambria*, broken up in 1925. *K.Turner Collection*

The *Cambria*'s slightly larger sister ship *Scotia*, launched in 1902 and broken up in 1928.

K.Turner Collection

4B

Belfast-owned twin-screw steamer *Heroic*, launched in 1906 to work the Liverpool – Belfast service. She was not broken up until 1952 after ending her days on the Liverpool – Dublin run.   *K. Turner Collection*

Lastly, two more LNWR twin-screw steamers: the 1898-built *Galtee More* (broken up in 1926)…

K. Turner Collection

… and sister ship *Connemara,* sadly sunk off Greenore in 1916, with no survivors, after she struck an unlit collier in a gale.   *K. Turner Collection*

MAP 5   **1 JANUARY 1920**

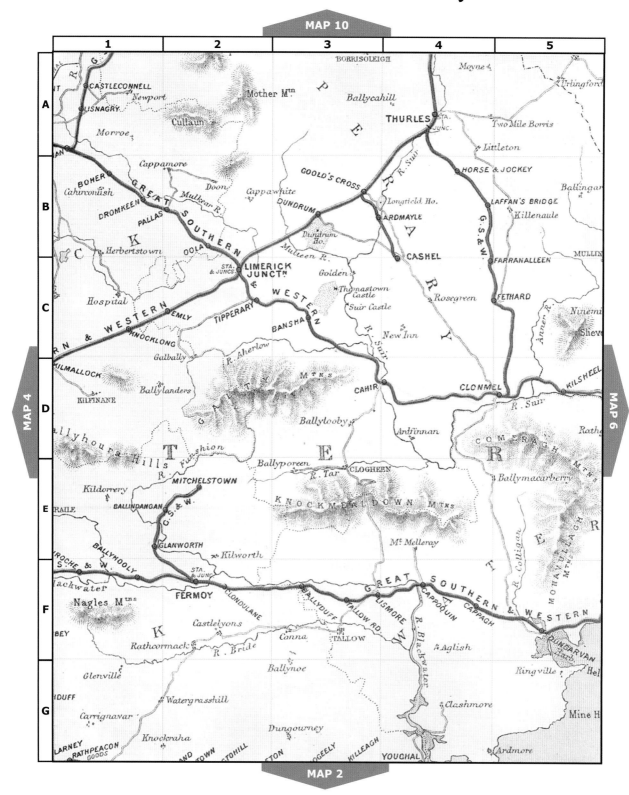

MAP 10
MAP 4
MAP 6
MAP 2

LEGEND

All lines 5ft 3in gauge

A1 LISNAGRY: Originally named NENAGH ROAD
B4 LAFFAN'S BRIDGE: Also known as LAFFAN'S BRIDGE & KILLENAULE
D5 POWERSTOWN PARK: An untimetabled halt existed here to serve
    Clonmel racecourse (See MAP 5A)
E2 BRIGOWN MILITARY PLATFORM: An untimetabled halt existed here
    to serve Kilworth army camp (See MAP 5A)
F1 DURROW: Full name was DURROW & STRADBALLY
F2 CLONDULANE: Originally named GLENWICK
G1 RATHPEACON: Only ever a freight facility

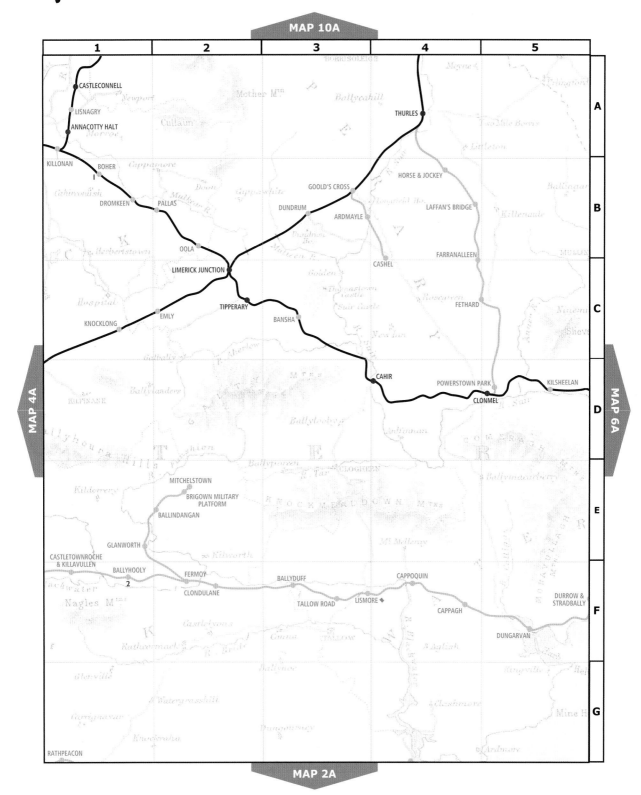

MAP 10A

MAP 4A

MAP 6A

MAP 2A

LEGEND

1 BOHER: Former station building now Boher Community Centre
2 BALLYHOOLY: Former goods shed now the Old Train House B&B. www.oldtrainhouse.com

Holiday Return Tickets

TO

DUBLIN

(WESTLAND ROW)

AND

Certain Stations on the Great Southern Railways (Ireland) via Holyhead and Kingstown (Dun Laoghaire)

WILL BE GIVEN ON

FRIDAYS AND SATURDAYS

From 1st April until 29th October
Also to Dublin on 20th, 21st, 22nd and 23rd June

BY TRAINS LEAVING

Aberdeen 1.0 p.m., Dumfries 7.26 p.m., Dundee (West) 2.50 p.m., Edinburgh (Princes Street) 5.35 p.m., Glasgow (Central) 5.30 p.m., Inverness 11.0 a.m., Perth 3.45 p.m. and Stirling 4.40 p.m.

See front page for Embarkation regulations during the International Eucharistic Congress in Dublin from 17th until 26th June, inclusive.

Passengers travelling on Saturdays, who cannot reach their destination on Sunday, may be allowed to go forward from Dublin on the Monday following date of issue.

RETURN ARRANGEMENTS

Passengers may return on any Sailing Day up to and including 16 days from date of issue, by any Ordinary Train in time to connect with Mail Steamer from Kingstown (Dun Laoghaire).

CHARGES FOR BERTHS ON STEAMERS

Holyhead and Kingstown Service.

Saloon—

	s.	d.	
Special State Rooms	15	0	including "made up" bed.
Awning Deck Cabins	7	6	
Main Deck Cabins	5	0	

Lower Deck Berths in Cabins and Open Berths, Free.
Charge of 2/6 each berth if "made up" bed provided.

Steerage—

Charge for Berths (including Rug and Pillow) ... 2 0

Passengers requiring berths on the Steamers should make early application to the undermentioned at the same time stating whether a Saloon or Steerage Berth is required, and send requisite fee.

From Ireland ... Irish Traffic Manager, L M S Rly., 15 Westmoreland Street, Dublin.
To Ireland ... Marine Superintendent, L M S Rly., Holyhead.

2

Detail from a 1932 LMS handbill promoting train and ferry services for holidaymakers from all parts of Scotland to Dublin and beyond...

... and the front of a similar 1938 handbill, this time targeting travellers going in the opposite direction to England and Wales as well as Scotland.

5C

MAP 6

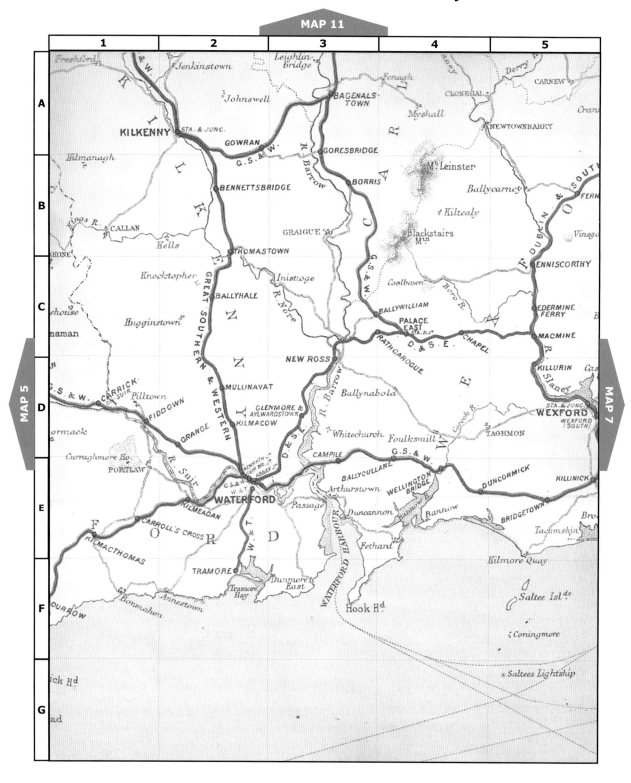

LEGEND

All lines 5ft 3in gauge

A3 BAGENALSTOWN: Originally named BAGNALSTOWN
B2 BENNETTSBRIDGE: Originally named BENNETSBRIDGE
C3 BALLYWILLIAM: Originally named BALLYWILLIAM FOR NEW ROSS
C4 CHAPEL: Also timetabled as CHAPEL FOR CLONROCHE
C5 MACMINE: Full name was MACMINE JUNCTION
D1 FIDDOWN: Also known as FIDDOWN & PORTLAW
D2 GRANGE: Renamed ANNACOTTY in 1928
D3 GLENMORE & AYLWARDSTOWN: Originally named AYLWARDSTOWN
D5 WEXFORD: Renamed WEXFORD NORTH in c1947
E2 WATERFORD stations were:
    WATERFORD THE MANOR [WATERFORD & TRAMORE RAILWAY]
    WATERFORD NORTH [other railways]
E5 KILLINICK: Originally named ORRISTOWN JUNCTION and then ASSALLY JUNCTION
F1 DURROW: Also known as DURROW & STRADBALLY

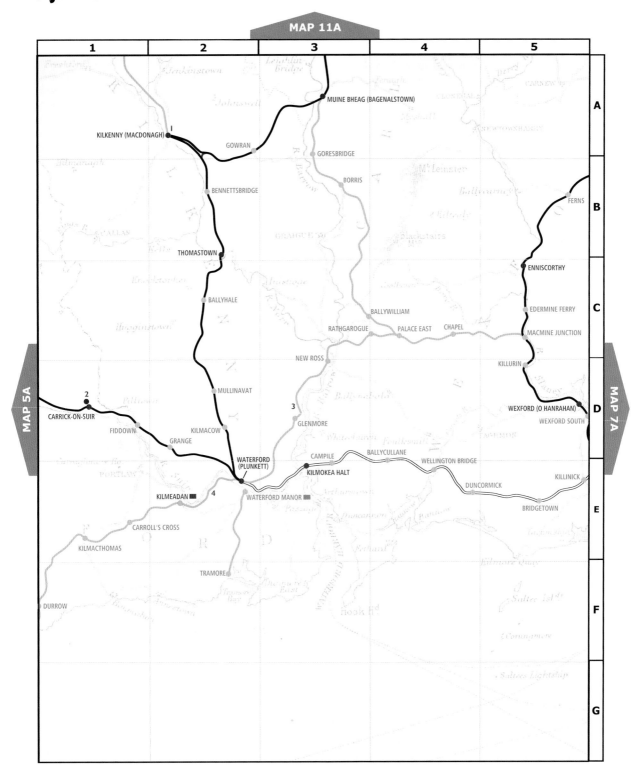

MAP 11A

MAP 5A

MAP 7A

	1	2	3	4	5

A
B
C
D
E
F
G

MUINE BHEAG (BAGENALSTOWN)

KILKENNY (MACDONAGH) 1

GOWRAN

GORESBRIDGE

BORRIS

FERNS

BENNETTSBRIDGE

ENNISCORTHY

THOMASTOWN

EDERMINE FERRY

BALLYHALE

BALLYWILLIAM

MACMINE JUNCTION

RATHGAROGUE   PALACE EAST   CHAPEL

NEW ROSS

KILLURIN

MULLINAVAT

WEXFORD (O HANRAHAN)

3

WEXFORD SOUTH

2

GLENMORE

CARRICK-ON-SUIR

FIDDOWN

KILMACOW

CAMPILE   BALLYCULLANE

WELLINGTON BRIDGE

KILLINICK

GRANGE

WATERFORD (PLUNKETT)

KILMOKEA HALT

DUNCORMICK

KILMEADAN   ▓   4   WATERFORD MANOR ▓

BRIDGETOWN

CARROLL'S CROSS

KILMACTHOMAS

TRAMORE

DURROW

LEGEND

1 KILKENNY (MACDONAGH): Current station is in the rebuilt goods shed. The original station buildings are now part of a shopping complex. www.macdonaghjunction.com

2 CARRICK-ON-SUIR: Former goods shed now operating base of the IRISH TRACTION GROUP. www.irishtractiongroup.com

3 NEW ROSS – WATERFORD: Former trackbed subject of narrow gauge railway plus cycleway proposal

4 3ft gauge WATERFORD & SUIR VALLEY RAILWAY. www.wsvrailway.ie

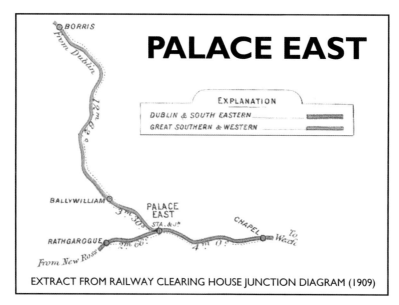

PALACE EAST

EXPLANATION

DUBLIN & SOUTH EASTERN ....
GREAT SOUTHERN & WESTERN ....

EXTRACT FROM RAILWAY CLEARING HOUSE JUNCTION DIAGRAM (1909)

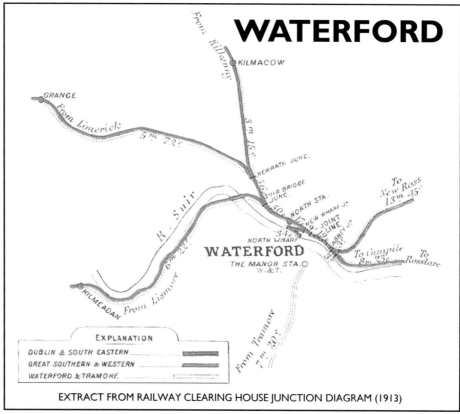

WATERFORD

EXPLANATION

DUBLIN & SOUTH EASTERN ....
GREAT SOUTHERN & WESTERN ....
WATERFORD & TRAMORE ....

EXTRACT FROM RAILWAY CLEARING HOUSE JUNCTION DIAGRAM (1913)

THE DUBLIN & SOUTH EASTERN RAILWAY

With 156 miles of routes and 100-plus locomotives, the Dublin & South Eastern Railway was a middling-sized system covering the townships and ports to the south of Dublin. It began as the Dublin & Kingstown Railway, opened on 17 December 1834, to which other railways were added gradually by different companies. Besides the DKR (which retained its nominal independence right up to the 1925 Amalgamation), the main forefather of the DSER was the 1846 Waterford, Wexford, Wicklow & Dublin Railway which, after a succession of line openings and name changes, on 1 January 1907 became the DSER. From its two Dublin termini (Harcourt Street and Westland Row) the railway's two northernmost lines met just north of Bray then continued south through Wicklow (1855) to the two southern termini of Wexford (1872) and Waterford (1904); a central 16½-mile branch ran inland to Shillelagh (1865).

In 1925 the DSER became part of the GSR, then later the CIE. Today only the Westland Row – now Dublin (Pearse) – to Wexford main line remains open, though since 30 June 2004 part of the old Harcourt Street line alignment has found a new use as the trackbed for part of the Luas tramway system's Green Line. One original DSER locomotive survives in preservation - in operational condition – at the RPSI's base at Whitehead: No.15 (later GSR 461), a Beyer, Peacock 2-6-0 of 1922 vintage.

A Valentine's postcard of Waterford's main station, looking south across the River Suir. *K.Turner Collection*

Waterford, Limerick & Western Railway No.15 *Roxborough*, an 0-4-0 tank engine built by the company in 1894 at Limerick. Incorporated in 1845 as the Waterford & Limerick Railway (with a subsequent name change in 1896), the company was absorbed by the GSWR in 1901. *K.Turner Collection*

THE WATERFORD & TRAMORE RAILWAY

In all respects save one the Waterford & Tramore Railway was very much a conventional standard gauge branch line – the one respect making it unique being that at no time in its life was it ever connected to any other railway. Incorporated under an Act of Parliament on 24 July 1851, it ran for 7¼ miles between the south bank of the River Suir in Waterford and the coastal resort of Tramore to the south; there were no intermediate stations. Opened on 6 September 1853, it passed in turn to the GSR and the CIE – who closed it on 31 December 1960. Motive power was supplied by a small (and constantly changing) mixed stud of ex-contractors' and other locomotives, bought or borrowed, followed, from late 1954 onwards, by three diesel railcars and two trailers.

MAP 7

1 JANUARY 1920

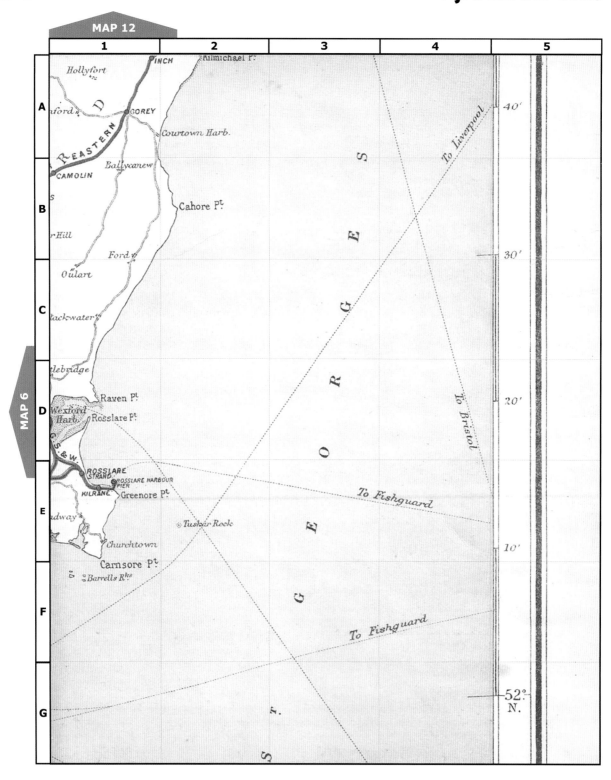

LEGEND

All lines 5ft 3in gauge

D1 – E1 Northern chord to the WEXFORD – ROSSLARE main line closed in 1918
E1 Name of pier station was ROSSLARE HARBOUR

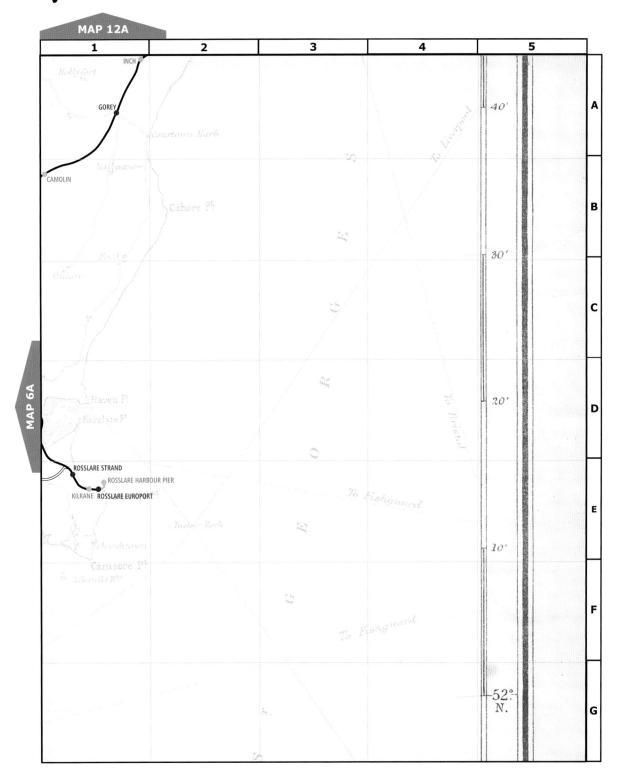

LEGEND

ROSSLARE EUROPORT (E1) is the latest in a succession of stations on, or
near this site, beginning with BALLYGEARY (opened 1971)

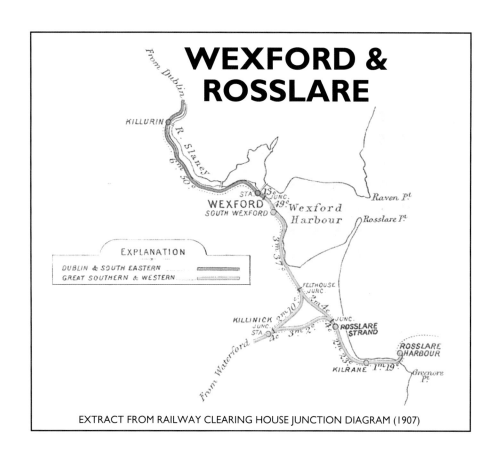

EXTRACT FROM RAILWAY CLEARING HOUSE JUNCTION DIAGRAM (1907)

Rosslare Strand station, as it looks today, with the abandoned line to Waterford disappearing left at the end of the platform.
Harry Maeers

Three postcard studies of very different locomotives from across Ireland. Firstly, a works photograph of GNR(I) 4-4-0 No.203 (to be named *Armagh*) built in 1948 by Beyer, Peacock of Manchester...
K.Turner Collection

...followed by another Beyer, Peacock product, BCDR 2-4-0 No.6 on a Leamington Spa-published postcard...

...and finally another works photograph, this time of one of the two large 4-6-2 narrow gauge tank engines built by Kerr, Stuart of Stoke-on-Trent in 1904 as Nos 9 and 10 of the LLSR.
K.Turner Collection

MAP 8

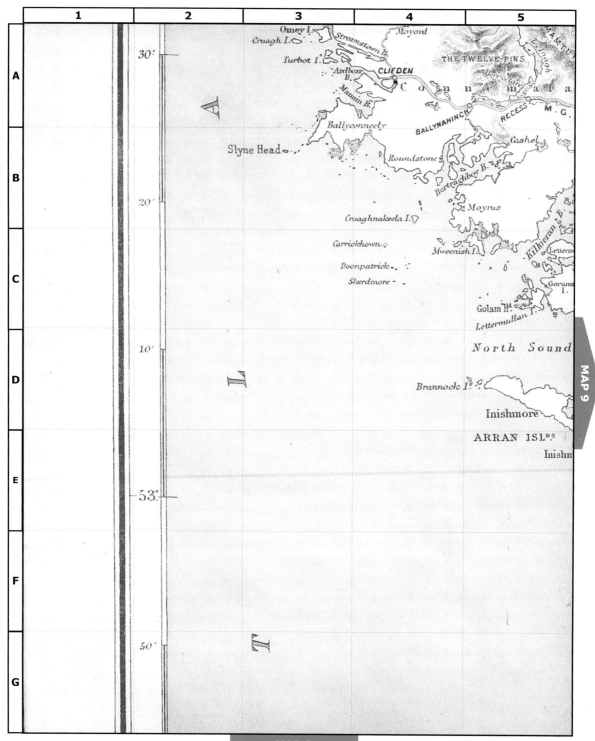

MAP 9

MAP 3

LEGEND

All lines 5ft 3in gauge

A5 RECESS HOTEL PLATFORM: A halt existed here 2 miles east of RECESS. (See MAP 8A)

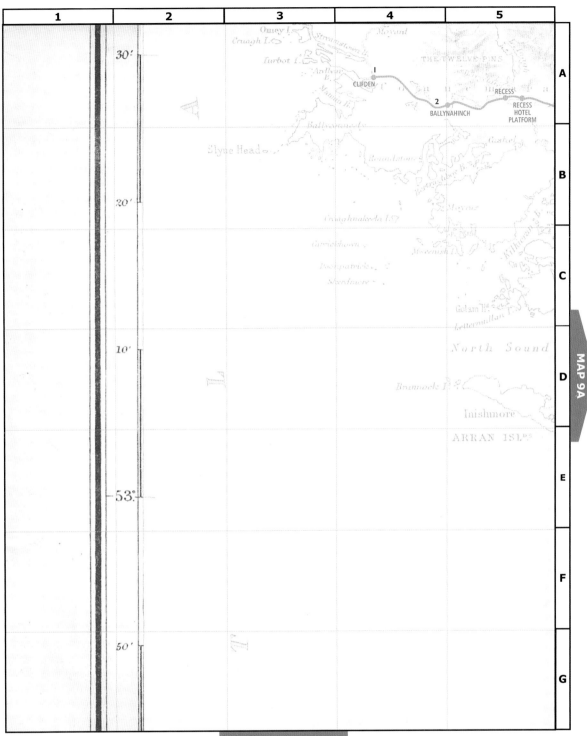

MAP 9A

MAP 3A

LEGEND

1 CLIFDEN: Station now part of an architectural complex including studio workshop and design centre, the Clifden Station House Hotel (www.clifdenstationhouse.com), and the Station House Museum in the former engine shed (www.radiomuseum.org)
2 CLIFDEN – OUGHTERARD planned for conversion into the CONNEMARA GREENWAY, part of the National Cycle Network

B 22468

GREAT
BRITAIN
and
NORTHERN
IRELAND

VIA STRANRAER
AND LARNE
THE SHORT SEA ROUTE

OPEN SEA PASSAGE
70 MINUTES

15th SEPTEMBER, 1957 until
8th JUNE 1958

BRITISH RAILWAYS

Sailing ticket arrangements

for travel between

GREAT BRITAIN
and NORTHERN
IRELAND

via

Heysham - Belfast

Next time—I'm gonna get a Sailing Ticket

JULY AND
AUGUST 1960

For full details of Steamer
Sailings and Principal Train
Services see separate folder

The fronts of two (folded) handbills, typical of their time, issued by British Railways in the 1950s and 1960s promoting alternative sea crossings to Ireland in the face of the growing threat from air travel.

TO AND FROM
NORTHERN IRELAND
VIA STRANRAER AND LARNE

TRAIN CONNECTIONS
AND
STEAMER SERVICES

15th September, 1957 until 8th June, 1958
(No Steamer Sailings on Sundays)

TO NORTHERN IRELAND

TRAIN		Nightly (Mondays to Fridays)	Sunday nights
London (Euston) ....leave		7K 30 p.m.	7 30 p.m.
Birmingham (New Street)...................... „		8A 20 p.m.	6A 25 p.m.
Manchester (Exchange)........................ „		10B 45 p.m.	11B 8 p.m.
Newcastle-on-Tyne (Central)................ „		J12D 30 a.m.	J12C 30 a.m.
Glasgow (St. Enoch) .... „		9 0 p.m.	8X 45 p.m.

STEAMER		Early Morning Mondays to Saturdays
Stranraer Harbour ....leave		7 0 a.m.
Larne Harbour............................arrive		9 15 a.m.

TRAIN		
Belfast (York Road)........................arrive		10 5 a.m.

FROM NORTHERN IRELAND

TRAIN		Nightly (Mondays to Saturdays)
Belfast (York Road)........................leave		5 55 p.m.

STEAMER		
Larne Harbour............................leave		6 50 p.m.
Stranraer Harbour ....arrive		8 55 p.m.

TRAIN		
Glasgow (St. Enoch)........................arrive		11 51 p.m.
Newcastle-on-Tyne (Central)........................ „		J4§ 2 a.m.
Manchester (Exchange)........................ „		J6§ 15 a.m.
Birmingham (New Street) .... „		G6§ 50 a.m.
London (Euston) .... „		8§ 10 a.m.

A—Change at Crewe.
B—Change at Wigan.
C—Early morning Mondays.
D—Early morning, Tuesdays to Saturdays.
G—Change at Crewe and on Sunday mornings arrives 6.33 a.m.
J—Change at Carlisle.
K—Departs 7.40 p.m. on Friday nights until 25th October, 1957, and from 23rd May, 1958.
X—From 29th September, 1957, until 11th May, 1958, leaves from Glasgow (Central) station.   §—Following day.

RESERVATION OF
SLEEPING BERTHS AND SEATS
ON TRAINS

Limited sleeping accommodation (first class, single berth compartments 40/-; second class 22/6 per berth) is available between London (Euston) and Stranraer Harbour. Seats can be reserved on certain of the principal connecting trains to and from Stranraer Harbour at a fee of two shillings per seat.

For reservations from London to Stranraer application should be made to the Station Master, Euston Station, London, N.W.1; and for reservations from Stranraer, to the Shipping Traffic Superintendent, 24 Donegall Place, Belfast.

Passengers who book sleeping berths and fail to use them will be required to pay the sleeping berth charge unless notice of cancellation is given before 4.0 p.m. on the day prior to that for which the berths are booked.

PASSENGER ORDINARY FARES
TO AND FROM NORTHERN IRELAND
(SUBJECT TO ALTERATION)

FROM OR TO	SINGLE FARES WITH LARNE HARBOUR			WITH BELFAST (York Rd.)		
	1st Cl.	2nd Cl. Rail, 1st in Ship	2nd Cl.	1st Cl.	2nd Cl. Rail, 1st in Ship	2nd Cl.
London (Euston)....................	123/3	91/5	77/11	130/5	96/2	82/8
Birmingham (New Street)......	98/8	75/-	61/6	105/10	79/9	66/3
Manchester (Exchange).........	81/5	62/11	50/-	88/5	64/8	52/8
Newcastle-on-Tyne (Central)	67/5	54/2	40/8	74/7	58/11	45/5
Glasgow (St. Enoch).............	50/6	41/9	29/10	53/6	43/10	31/7
Stranraer Harbour	27/9 1st Cl.		14/3 2nd Cl.	34/11	32/6	19/-

FROM OR TO	RETURN FARES WITH LARNE HARBOUR			WITH BELFAST (York Rd.)		
	1st Cl.	2nd Cl. Rail, 1st in Ship	2nd Cl.	1st Cl.	2nd Cl. Rail, 1st in Ship	2nd Cl.
London (Euston).................	237/5	176/9	149/9	247/10	184/2	158/-
Birmingham (New Street)......	190/2	145/4	118/4	205/2	152/4	126/6
Manchester (Exchange).........	153/9	124/4	97/4	167/5	129/4	105/2
Newcastle-on-Tyne (Central)	134/10	108/4	81/4	147/3	116/7	89/7
Glasgow (St. Enoch).............	101/-	82/9	58/5	103/5	82/9	58/5
Stranraer Harbour	55/6 1st Cl.		28/6 2nd Cl.	67/11	63/9	36/9

Holders of SECOND CLASS tickets may travel 1st Class in Ship on payment of the difference between the 2nd Class and 1st Class fares.

SLEEPING ACCOMMODATION
ON BOARD THE STEAMER

To Larne.
7.0 a.m. Mail Service.—Passengers to Ireland may sleep on board at Stranraer from 10.0 p.m. until arrival at Larne 9.0 a.m. next day (Saturday nights excepted).

From Larne.
6.50 p.m. Mail Service.—Passengers from Ireland may sleep on board at Stranraer until 6.30 a.m. next day (Saturday nights excepted).

CHARGES.—The charges for Cabin and Berth accommodation, which are subject to alteration, are additional to the First or Second Class fares, and are as follows:—

FIRST CLASS
SPECIAL CABIN (without Toilet or Bath).
    One Passenger 32/6
    Two Passengers 40/-
SINGLE CABIN 16/-
BERTH IN 2-BERTH CABIN 8/-

SECOND CLASS
BERTH IN 2, 4 OR 6-BERTH CABIN 6/-
OPEN BERTH { MADE-UP BED 5/-
            { RUG AND PILLOW 4/6

Passengers requiring cabins or berths on the steamer should make early application, giving full particulars, including class of berth required, and at the same time enclose the requisite fee. Reservations cannot be effected until the berth fees are paid.

Passengers booking berths and subsequently desiring to cancel the reservations are required to give notice as under:—

For sailings between 6.0 p.m. and midnight } Not later than 10.30 a.m. on the day of sailing.

For sailings between midnight and 6.0 p.m. } Not later than 10.30 a.m. on the day previous to the day of sailing.

Unless such notice is given, applications for the refund of berth and cabin fees cannot be entertained.

Meals and Refreshments can be obtained on the steamer.

Applications for cabin accommodation for sailings in both directions should be addressed to:—

District Marine Manager, British Railways, Stranraer Harbour.
Telegraphic Address: " Marine Rail, Stranraer."
Telephone No. 49.

A limited number of berths can also be booked at Euston station, London and St. Enoch station, Glasgow, on personal application.

The reverse of the British Railways 1957/58 handbill, detailing all the prospective passenger needed to know in order to plan his or her journey via Stranraer from elsewhere in England or Scotland.

MAP 9

I JANUARY 1920

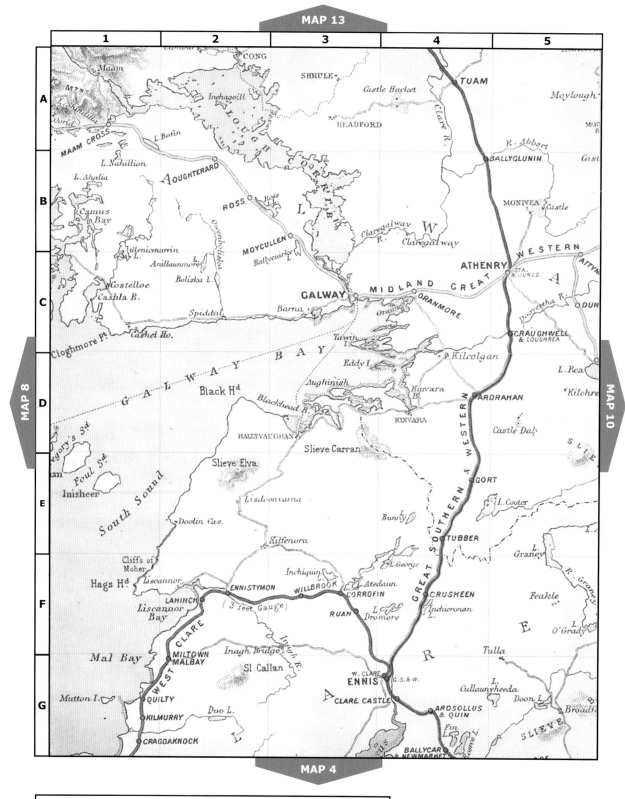

MAP 13
MAP 8
MAP 10
MAP 4

LEGEND

All lines 5ft 3in gauge except:
3ft gauge WEST CLARE RAILWAY (G1 – G4)

C5 ATTYMON: Correct name was ATTYMON JUNCTION; originally named ATTYMON
F2 LAHINCH: Also timetabled as LEHINCH
F2 WORKHOUSE HALT: An untimetabled workhouse staff halt existed midway between LAHINCH and ENNISTYMON.
    It closed in 1925 but reopened as a railcar halt on 29 June 1953 (See MAP 9A)
F3 CORROFIN: Correct name was COROFIN
G1 KILMURRY: Originally named KILMURRY & MULLARGH
G2 MILTOWN MALBAY: Also timetabled as MILTOWN-MALBAY
G4 BALLYCAR & NEWMARKET: Correct name was BALLYCAR; originally named BALLYCAR & NEWMARKET
G4 ENNIS: Station shared by the GSWR and the WCR

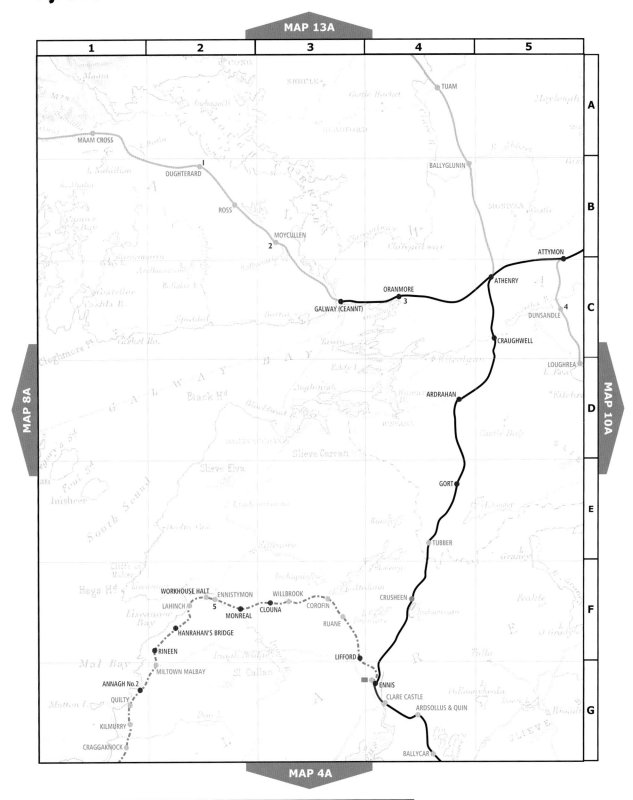

MAP 13A

	1	2	3	4	5	

MAP 8A

MAP 10A

MAP 4A

LEGEND

1 OUGHTERARD: Now a carpet factory. www.thedixoncarpetcompany.com
2 MOYCULLEN: Site now occupied by a crystal glass factory. www.celticcrystalireland.com
3 ORANMORE: New station (opened 2013) located ¾ mile west of the old station (closed 1963)
4 DUNSANDLE: Station privately restored as the base for a railway heritage centre. www.dunsandlerailwaystation.com
5 ENNISTYMON: Former station building now incorporated into a large guest house. www.bb-stationhouse.com

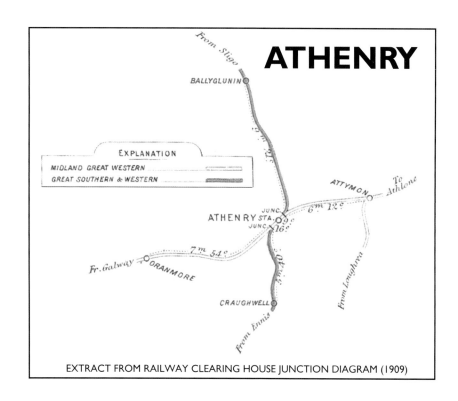

EXTRACT FROM RAILWAY CLEARING HOUSE JUNCTION DIAGRAM (1909)

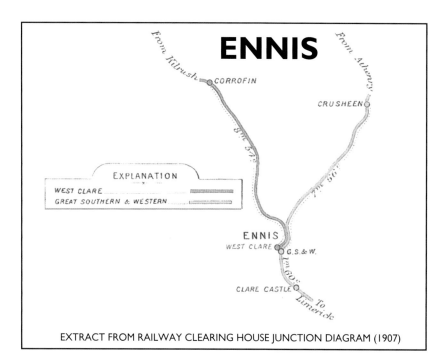

EXTRACT FROM RAILWAY CLEARING HOUSE JUNCTION DIAGRAM (1907)

9B

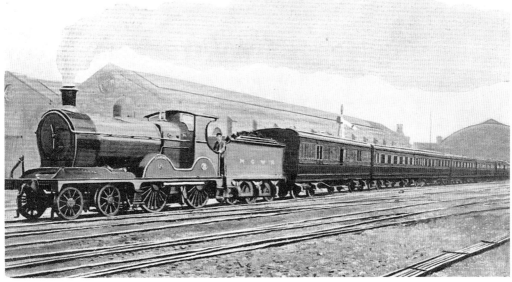

A Valentine's 'artistic' postcard of an MGWR passenger train, headed by one of the company's many 4-4-0 locomotives in its distinctive pre-1914 emerald green livery.   *K.Turner Collection*

THE WEST CLARE RAILWAY

The West Clare Railway was, in actual fact, formed of two 3ft gauge railways worked as one: the West Clare and the South Clare. Both companies were incorporated in 1884 under the provisions of the 1883 Tramways (Ireland) Act; the first ran from Ennis to Milton Malbay (opened 2 July 1887) while the second ran from Milton Malbay to termini at Kilrush and Kilkee via the triangular Moyasta Junction. The short Kilrush – Kilree section opened on 13 August 1892 and the connection back north to Milton Malbay on 23 December that year. Total route length of the single-track system was some 53 miles, the whole being worked by a fleet of tank engines and, in later years, diesel locomotives and railcars.

Control of the railway passed in 1925 to the GSR, then in turn to the CIE – who closed the entire system down on 31 January 1961. A small section however has been restored as a heritage line at Moyasta Junction, home to WCR No.5 *Slieve Callan*, an 0-6-2 tank built in 1892 by Dübs of Glasgow.

THE MIDLAND GREAT WESTERN RAILWAY

With nearly 540 miles of route, the Midland Great Western Railway was, at its greatest extent, the third largest railway in Ireland. Incorporated by Act of Parliament on 21 July 1845, it began life with a 26-mile stretch of line from Dublin Broadside station westwards to Enfield, opened on 28 July 1847; thereafter the line slowly advanced, firstly (on 6 December 1847) to Kinnegad – later renamed Hill of Down – then Mullingar (2 October 1848) and finally Galway (1 August 1851), 126 miles from Dublin.

Other main lines, branches and absorptions of smaller concerns followed, and running powers over other companies' metals obtained. Sligo was added to the system on 3 September 1862, at the end of a long line from Mullingar, while Westport on the coast between Sligo and Galway was reached on 24 January 1866. All three of these main lines remain open, though most of the branches have been closed following the system's becoming part of firstly the GSR and then the CIE.

During its lifetime the MGWR owned nearly 300 locomotives and, uniquely for a stud of that size, virtually all were named. It also owned the Royal Canal, linking Dublin with the River Shannon, and leased the rival Grand Canal, which linked Dublin to the Shannon further downstream.

MAP 10

1 JANUARY 1920

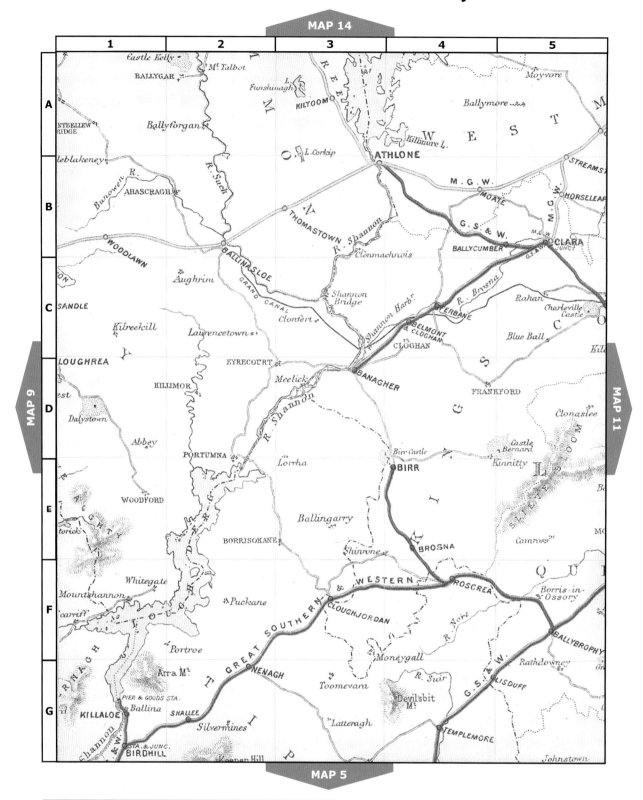

MAP 14

MAP 9

MAP 11

MAP 5

LEGEND

All lines 5ft 3in gauge

B1 WOODLAWN: Also known as WOODLAWN FOR LOUGHREA
B4 BALLINAHOUN: An untimetabled race traffic halt existed between ATHLONE and CLARA;
    originally named DOON; also known as BALLINAHOWN. (See MAP 10A)
B5 BALLYCUMBER: Originally named PROSPECT
E4 BIRR: Originally named PARSONSTOWN
E4 BROSNA: Also known as BROSNA HALT
F5 BALLYBROPHY: Originally named BORRIS & ROSCREA
G1 KILLALOE PIER: Pier extension used for trains meeting Lough Derg steamers
G4 LISDUFF: Also known as LISDUFF (KNOCKAHAW)

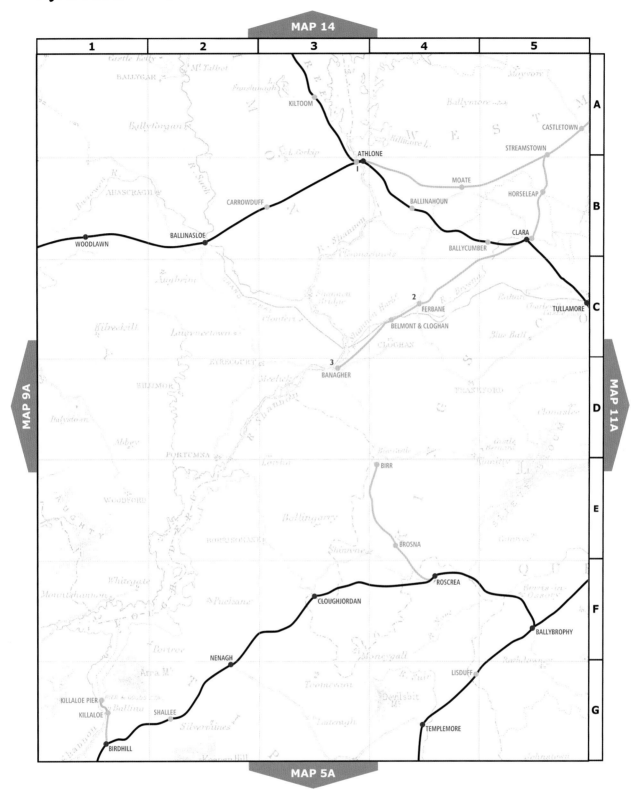

MAP 14

| | 1 | 2 | 3 | 4 | 5 | |

KILTOOM

CASTLETOWN

STREAMSTOWN

A

ATHLONE

MOATE

HORSELEAP

CARROWDUFF

BALLINAHOUN

B

WOODLAWN

BALLINASLOE

CLARA

BALLYCUMBER

TULLAMORE

C

2
FERBANE

BELMONT & CLOGHAN

CLOGHAN

3
BANAGHER

D

BIRR

E

BROSNA

ROSCREA

CLOUGHJORDAN

BALLYBROPHY

F

NENAGH

LISDUFF

KILLALOE PIER

KILLALOE

SHALLEE

G

BIRDHILL

TEMPLEMORE

MAP 9A

MAP 11A

MAP 5A

LEGEND

1 ATHLONE: Former MGWR station building now IE stores and offices
2 FERBANE: Former station building and goods shed now county council offices
3 BANAGHER: Site cleared as part of a marina

ATHLONE & CLARA

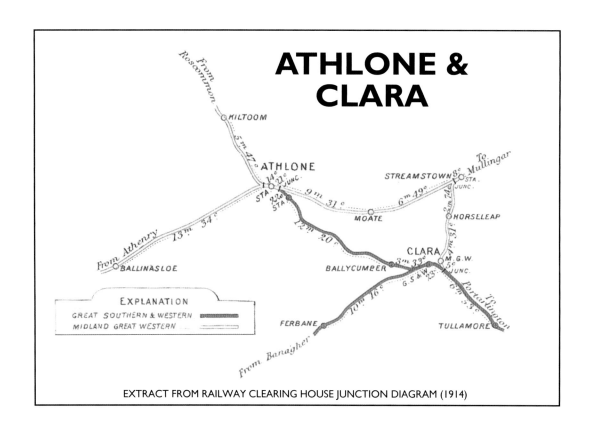

EXTRACT FROM RAILWAY CLEARING HOUSE JUNCTION DIAGRAM (1914)

Three more official LNWR postcards, sold in sets to holidaymakers and other tourists and featuring the major buildings, ruins and scenic attractions of Ireland. This is the former Viceregal Lodge in Dublin, once the summer residence of the Lord Lieutenant of Ireland but now the official residence of the Irish President.　　*K.Turner Collection*

The Meeting Bridge at Avoca with Moore's Tree beside it, under which the poet Thomas Moore wrote the song 'The Meeting of the Waters' about the rivers Avonmore and Avonbeg. The stump of the tree can still be seen here today.

K.Turner Collection

Promenading at Bray, on the town's mile-long seafront. Still a popular resort today, it happily retains its railway station, making it a favourite destination for daytrippers from Dublin.

K.Turner Collection

MAP 11

1 JANUARY 1920

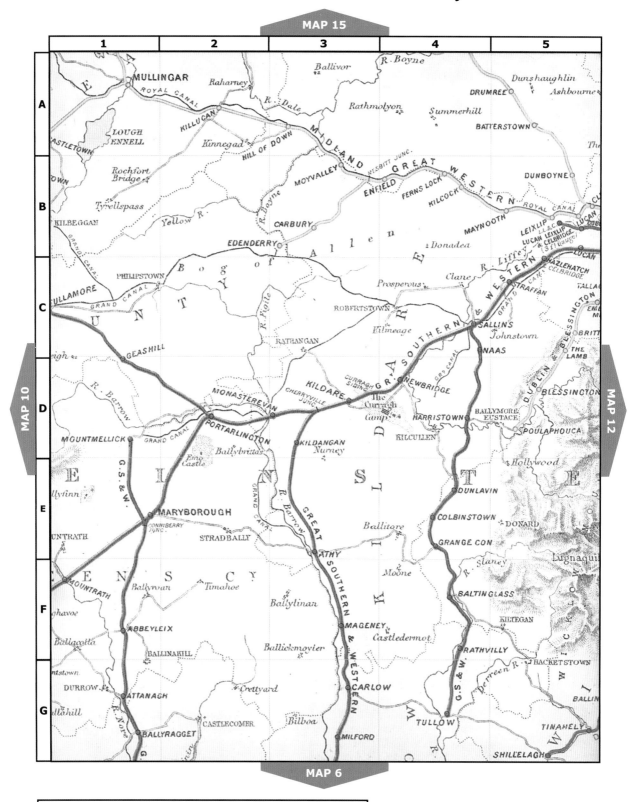

MAP 15

MAP 10

MAP 12

MAP 6

LEGEND

All lines 5ft 3in gauge except:
3ft 6in gauge DUBLIN & LUCAN ELECTRIC RAILWAY (B5)
3ft gauge LUCAN, LEIXLIP & CELBRIDGE STEAM TRAMWAY (B5) defunct at this date

A1 NEWBROOK RACECOURSE: A halt for race traffic existed 1¼ miles west of MULLINGAR. (See MAP 11A)
A3 HILL OF DOWN: Originally named KINNEGAD & BALLIVOR
A5 FAIRYHOUSE BRIDGE: A halt for race traffic existed 2¼ miles north of DUNBOYNE and used by regular
    traffic from 1931 onwards. (See MAP 11A)
B3 CARBURY: Originally named CARBERRY
B5 LEIXLIP [MGWR]: Originally named LOUISA BRIDGE & LEIXLIP
B5: LUCAN [MGWR]: Originally named COLDBLOW & or FOR LUCAN; also known as LUCAN NORTH
D3 Untimetabled halts sited at CURRAGH MAINLINE (race traffic only) and CURRAGH SIDING (also known
    as CURRAGH RACECOURSE PLATFORM for race traffic and military specials) between KILDARE and
    NEWBRIDGE. (See MAP 11A)
F1 MOUNTRATH: Correct name was MOUNTRATH & CASTLETOWN

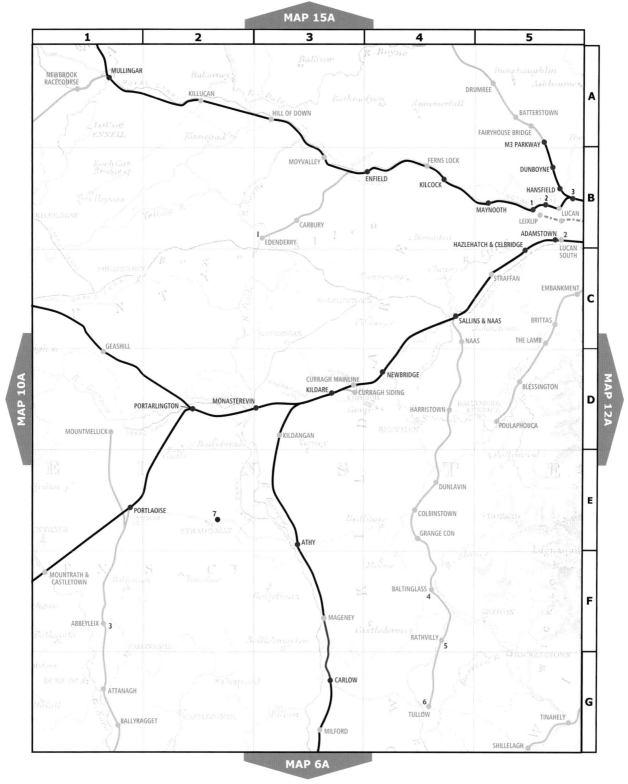

MAP 15A

MAP 10A

MAP 12A

MAP 6A

LEGEND

1 EDENDERRY: Former goods shed home to a car valeting business
2 LUCAN SOUTH: Renamed from LUCAN [GSWR] before closure (1963)
3 ABBEYLEIX: Former goods shed and yard now part of an industrial estate
4 BALTINGLAS: Now part of an industrial estate
5 RATHVILLY: Former goods shed now an industrial unit
6 TULLOW: Former goods shed now part of an industrial estate
7 IRISH STEAM PRESERVATION SOCIETY: Steam museum and 3ft gauge
    railway at Stradbally Hall. www.irishsteam.ie

THE DUBLIN & BLESSINGTON STEAM TRAMWAY

The Dublin & Blessington Steam Tramway, authorised by an 1880 Order-in-Council was, as its name suggests, a roadside steam tramway running south-west from the outskirts of Dublin to the town of Blessington 16½ miles away. Unusually for a line of this type, a gauge of 5ft 3in instead of 3ft was chosen in order to permit through running onto the Dublin United tramways street system – though in the event only goods and not passenger workings did so. The opening date was 1 August 1888.

Operated by the Dublin & Blessington Steam Tramway Company, the tramway was in effect extended nearly 5 miles on 1 May 1895 by the Blessington & Poulaphouca Steam Tramway Company to the beauty spot of its title, this line being worked by the the DBST. The extension closed on 30 September 1927 with the original portion of the tramway following on 31 December 1932 (having been owned for the last five years of its life by a Joint Committee of Dublin Corporation and the Dublin and Wicklow County Councils). Passenger working was originally with steam tramway locomotives hauling double-deck trailers; these were joined later by a variety of internal-combustion-powered passenger vehicles – one of which, a 1926 Drewry railcar, is preserved in the Ulster Folk & Transport Museum, Cultra, having worked (in 3ft gauge form) for the CDJC after the closure of the DBST.

THE DUBLIN & LUCAN ELECTRIC RAILWAY

Opened on 8 March 1900 under an 1897 Order-in-Council, the Dublin & Lucan Electric Railway was an electrified reconstruction of a 3ft 6in gauge roadside steam tramway (opened, in stages from 1 June 1880, as the 3ft gauge Dublin & Lucan Steam Tramway) running westwards for 7 miles from the outskirts of Dublin to the town of Lucan. Current was supplied, in conventional electric tramway fashion, via an overhead wire. In early 1925 the owners – the Dublin & Lucan Electric Railway Company – went bankrupt and on 29 January that year the line closed. It was taken over, from 7 July 1927, by the Dublin United Tramways for relaying and absorption as part of its standard gauge network.

THE LUCAN, LEIXLIP & CELBRIDGE STEAM TRAMWAY

Although the full route of the Lucan, Leixlip & Celbridge Steam Tramway is marked on the 1920 RCH Map, only part of it was open at that time – and then in a different guise. The LLCST, opened in June 1890 (exact date unknown), was no more than a 1½-mile 3ft gauge steam tramway extension of the DLST from the Lucan terminus to the village of Leixlip, the planned branch to Celbridge never being constructed. The line was worked by the DLST as part of its own line and closed with it early in 1900, but was not rebuilt and electrified – apart from a short section in 1912. (See the LLER below).

THE LUCAN & LEIXLIP ELECTRIC RAILWAY

In 1912 (exact date unknown) the Lucan & Leixlip Eletric Railway Company opened a ½-mile extension of the DLER, from its Lucan terminus to the village of Dodsboro', along the first part of the trackbed of the defunct LLCST. This short line was worked by the DLER under lease, and closed with that line in 1925 – though unlike that line was not rebuilt as a conventional tramway.

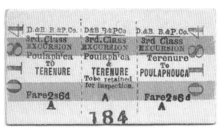

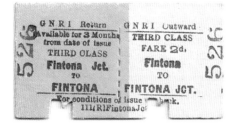

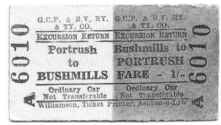
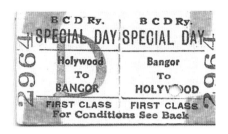

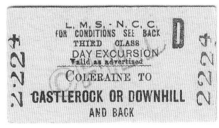

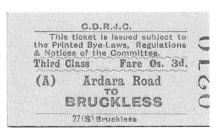
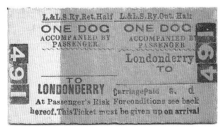

Just some of the immense variety of Irish railway tickets produced down the years, now very much collectable items of transport and social history interest in their own right.

MAP 12

1 JANUARY 1920

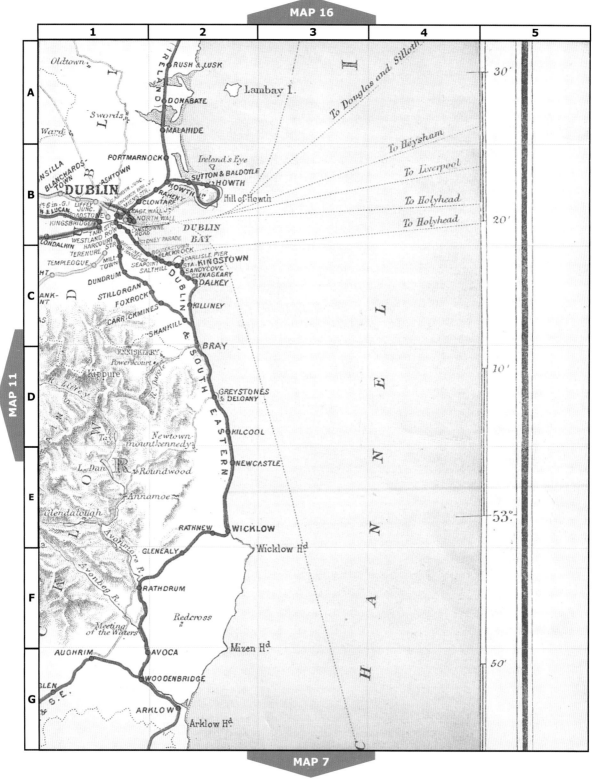

LEGEND

All lines 5ft 3in gauge except:
3ft 6in gauge DUBLIN & LUCAN ELECTRIC RAILWAY (B1)

B1 DLT terminus was in CONYNGHAM ROAD (See MAP 12A)
B1 INCHICORE RAILWAY WORKS: A workers' platform existed here, opening and closing dates unknown. (See MAP 12A)
B1 LANSDOWNE ROAD: Originally named LANSDOWNE ROAD & BALLSBRIDGE
B1 TARA STREET: Originally named TARA STREET & GEORGE'S QUAY
B2 HOWTH JUNCTION: Originally named JUNCTION
B2 SUTTON & BALDOYLE: Originally named BALDOYLE & SUTTON
B2 Southern loop between SUTTON & BALDOYLE and HOWTH formed by the GNR(I)'s standard gauge HILL OF HOWTH TRAMWAY
C2 FOXROCK: Originally named LEOPARDSTOWN; also timetabled as FOXROCK FOR LEOPARDSTOWN
C2 KILLINEY: Full name was KILLINEY & BALLYBRACK
C2 KINGSTOWN: Originally named KINGSTOWN HARBOUR
C2 SHANKILL: Also timetabled as SHANKILL (BRAY)
C2 WOODBROOK: A golf course halt existed north of BRAY
D2 GREYSTONES & DELGANY: Correct name was GREYSTONES; originally named DELGANY, then GREYSTONES & DELGANY
D2 KILCOOL: Originally named KILCOOLE & NEWTOWNMOUNTKENNEDY
E2 RATHNEW: Correct name was RATHNEW FOR NEWRATH BRIDGE; originally named NEWRATH BRIDGE, then RATHNEW (NEWRATH BRIDGE)
E2 WICKLOW MURROUGH: The original Wicklow terminus remained in use for goods and excursion traffic. (See MAP 12A)
G1 AVOCA: Originally named OVOCA
G1 WOODENBRIDGE: Full name was WOODENBRIDGE JUNCTION; originally named WOODENBRIDGE & SHILLELAGH JUNCTION

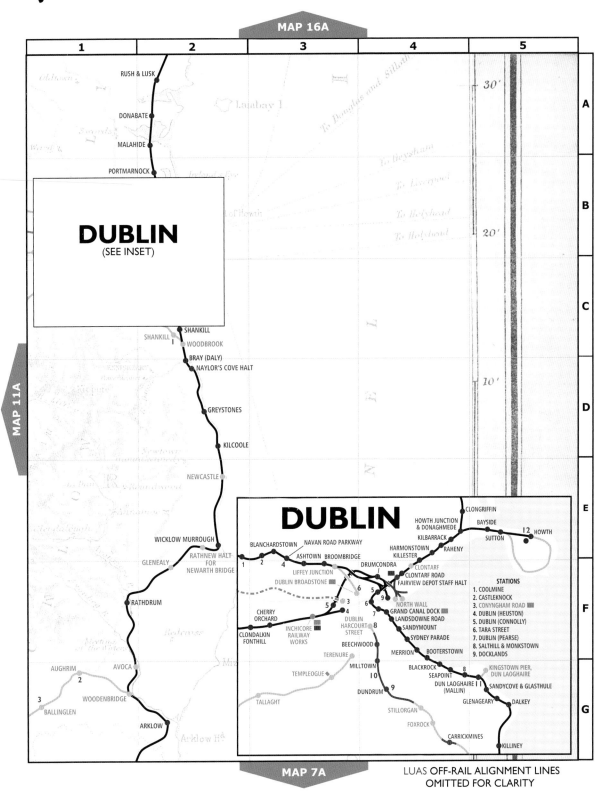

MAP 16A

MAP 11A

MAP 7A

LUAS OFF-RAIL ALIGNMENT LINES
OMITTED FOR CLARITY

RUSH & LUSK
DONABATE
MALAHIDE
PORTMARNOCK

DUBLIN
(SEE INSET)

SHANKILL
SHANKILL
WOODBROOK
BRAY (DALY)
NAYLOR'S COVE HALT

GREYSTONES

KILCOOLE

NEWCASTLE

WICKLOW MURROUGH

GLENEALY
RATHNEW HALT
FOR
NEWARTH BRIDGE

RATHDRUM

AUGHRIM
AVOCA
2
3
WOODENBRIDGE
BALLINGLEN
ARKLOW

DUBLIN

CLONGRIFFIN
HOWTH JUNCTION
& DONAGHMEDE
BAYSIDE
KILBARRACK
12 HOWTH
SUTTON
HARMONSTOWN
KILLESTER
RAHENY

BLANCHARDSTOWN
NAVAN ROAD PARKWAY
ASHTOWN
BROOMBRIDGE
DRUMCONDRA
1
2
LIFFEY JUNCTION
CLONTARF
DUBLIN BROADSTONE
CLONTARF ROAD
FAIRVIEW DEPOT STAFF HALT

6
5
9
NORTH WALL
GRAND CANAL DOCK
LANDSDOWNE ROAD
SANDYMOUNT
SYDNEY PARADE

CHERRY
ORCHARD
5
3
4
DUBLIN
HARCOURT
STREET
7
8
CLONDALKIN
FONTHILL
INCHICORE
RAILWAY
WORKS
BEECHWOOD
MERRION
BOOTERSTOWN
TERENURE

TEMPLEOGUE
MILLTOWN
BLACKROCK
SEAPOINT
8
KINGSTOWN PIER,
DUN LAOGHAIRE
10
DUN LAOGHAIRE 11
(MALLIN)
SANDYCOVE & GLASTHULE
DUNDRUM
9
GLENAGEARY
DALKEY
TALLAGHT
STILLORGAN
FOXROCK
CARRICKMINES
KILLINEY

STATIONS
1. COOLMINE
2. CASTLEKNOCK
3. CONYNGHAM ROAD
4. DUBLIN (HEUSTON)
5. DUBLIN (CONNOLLY)
6. TARA STREET
7. DUBLIN (PEARSE)
8. SALTHILL & MONKSTOWN
9. DOCKLANDS

1   2   3   4   5

A
B
C
D
E
F
G

30'
20'
10'

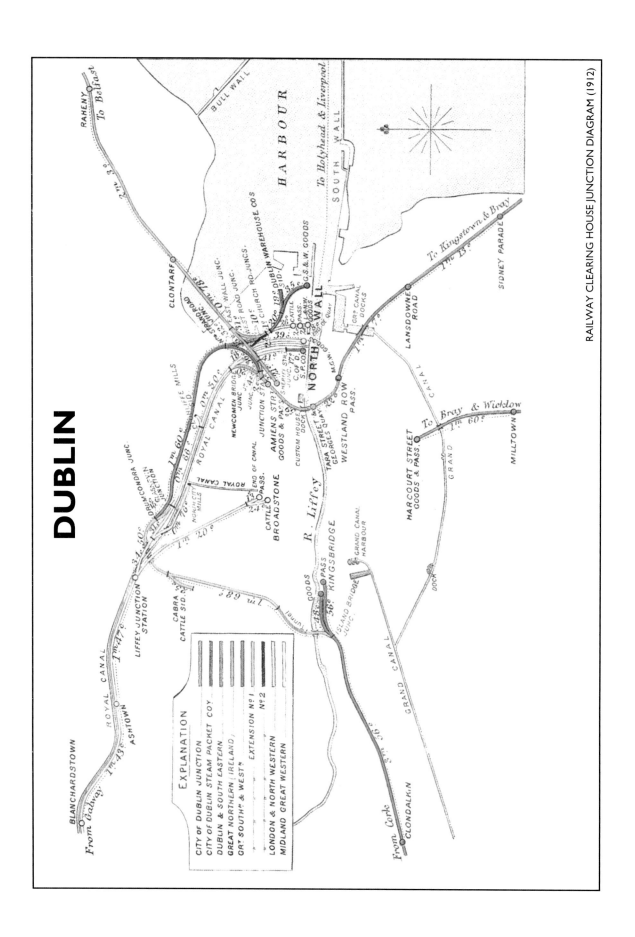

DUBLIN

RAILWAY CLEARING HOUSE JUNCTION DIAGRAM (1912)

EXPLANATION

CITY OF DUBLIN JUNCTION
CITY OF DUBLIN STEAM PACKET COY.
DUBLIN & SOUTH EASTERN
GREAT NORTHERN (IRELAND)
GRT SOUTHN & WESTN
    EXTENSION No.1
    No.2
LONDON & NORTH WESTERN
MIDLAND GREAT WESTERN

HHT No.9 (Milnes of 1902), lettered GREAT NORTHERN RAILWAY and in that company's painted teak livery. It was the tramway's official 'Last Car'. *K.Turner Collection*

THE HILL OF HOWTH TRAMWAY

The Hill of Howth Tramway was a standard gauge overhead electric tramway owned and operated by the GNR(I). Authorised by the Great Northern Railway (Ireland) Act 1897, it ran for just over 5 miles from the GNR(I)'s Sutton & Baldoyle station up to the summit of Slievemartin (opened 17 June 1901) and then down to Howth station (reached 1 August 1901). The tramway was worked with ten open-top double-deck cars, no less than four of which survive in preservation: No.2 in California, No.4 in the Ulster Folk & Transport Museum at Cultra, No.9 in the National Transport Museum at Howth Castle and No.10 at the National Tramway Museum at Crich in England.

Bray, Co. Wicklow

An undated Valentine's postcard of Bray station, looking south towards the 792ft-high Bray Head, which the railway skirts in spectacular fashion. *K.Turner Collection*

MAP 13

1 JANUARY 1920

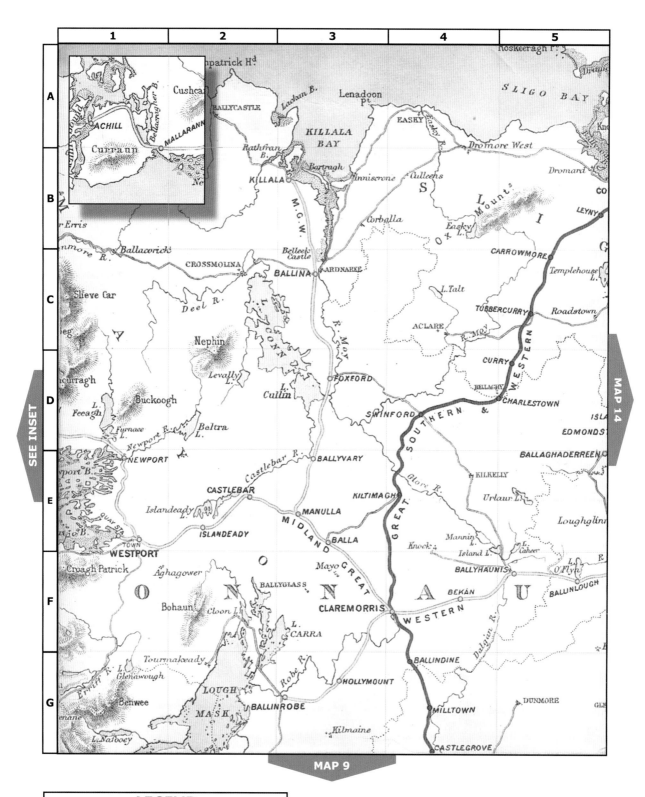

SEE INSET

MAP 14

MAP 9

LEGEND

All lines 5ft 3in gauge

E1 The two Westport stations were named WESTPORT QUAY and WESTPORT
    (formerly also WESTPORT TOWN)
E1 WESTPORT QUAY branch was freight-only post-1912
E3 MANULLA: Full name was MANULLA JUNCTION
G4 MILLTOWN: Also timetabled as MILLTOWN (GALWAY)

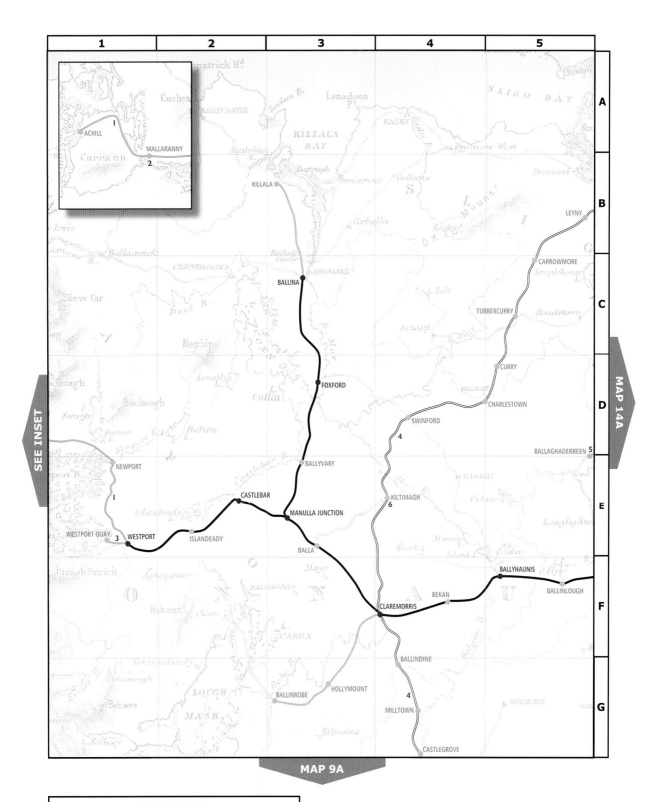

LEGEND

1 GREAT WESTERN GREENWAY (part of the National Cycle Network).
   www.greenway.ie
2 MALLARANNY: Station building being refurbished as a cafe/tearoom
3 WESTPORT GREENWAY. www.mayowalks.ie
4 Line mothballed against envisaged reopening as part of the Western Rail
   Corridor Project
5 BALLAGHADERREEN: Part of site occupied by a health centre; goods shed
   now Gaelic Athletic Association premises
6 KILTIMAGH: Former buildings now the Kiltimagh Museum of Local History.
   www.museumsofmayo.com

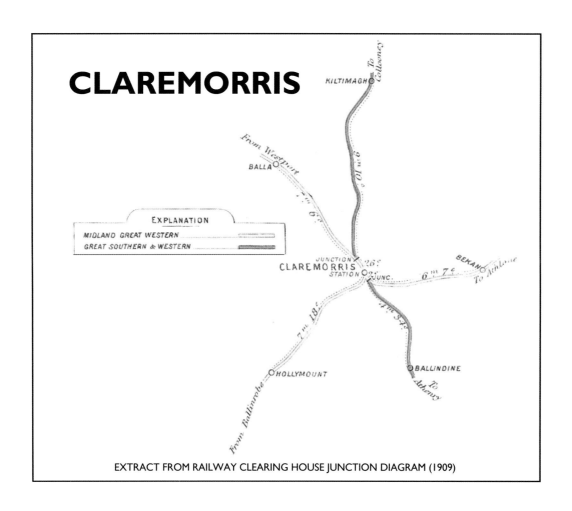

CLAREMORRIS

EXTRACT FROM RAILWAY CLEARING HOUSE JUNCTION DIAGRAM (1909)

A further trio of official LNWR postcards aimed at the tourist market: Kingstown Harbour, with the railway/steamer terminal on the far right...   *K.Turner Collection*

… the Eagle's Nest, a 1,100ft conical hill near Killarney, just south of…

…the Middle or Muckross Lake, one of the three famous Lakes of Killarney situated immediately south-west of the town.

MAP 14

1 JANUARY 1920

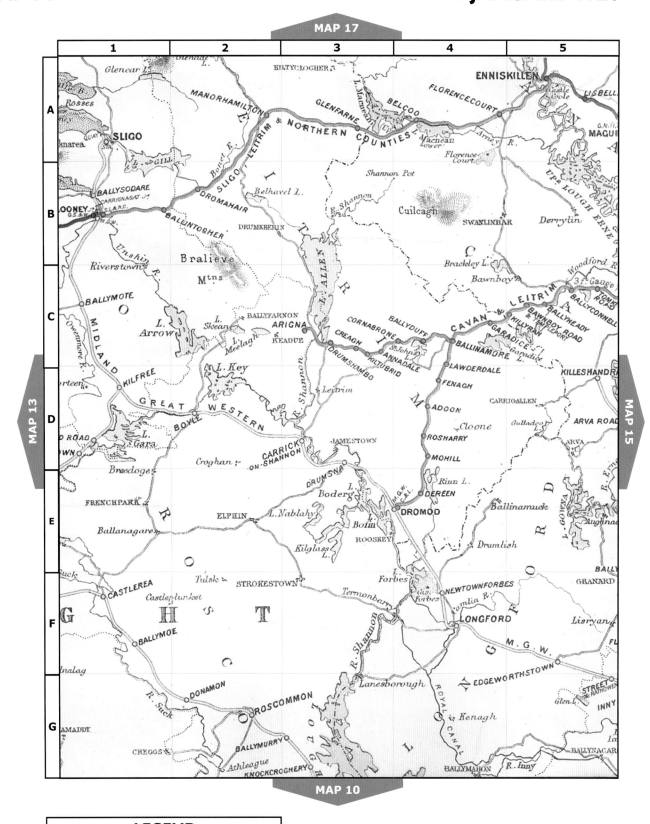

MAP 17
MAP 13
MAP 15
MAP 10

LEGEND

All lines 5ft 3in gauge except:
3ft gauge CAVAN & LEITRIM RAILWAY (C4 – E4 & C3 – C5)

A1 SLIGO quay line freight-only
A4 ABOHILL: An untimetabled station existed midway between
    BELCOO and FLORENCECOURT. (See Map 14A)
A4 BELCOO: Also known as BELCOO & BLACKLION
A5 MAGUIRESBRIDGE: Formerly MAGUIRE'S BRIDGE
B1 BALLYGAWLEY: An untimetabled halt (also known as BALLYGAWLEY
    MARKET PLATFORM) existed here. (See MAP 14A)
C3 DRUMSHAMBO: Correct station name was DRUMSHANBO
C3 DRINEY (also known as DRINEY CURVE) between KILTUBRID and
    ANNADALE was a halt used by excursion trains only. (See MAP 14A)
D1 KILFREE: Correct station name was KILFREE JUNCTION

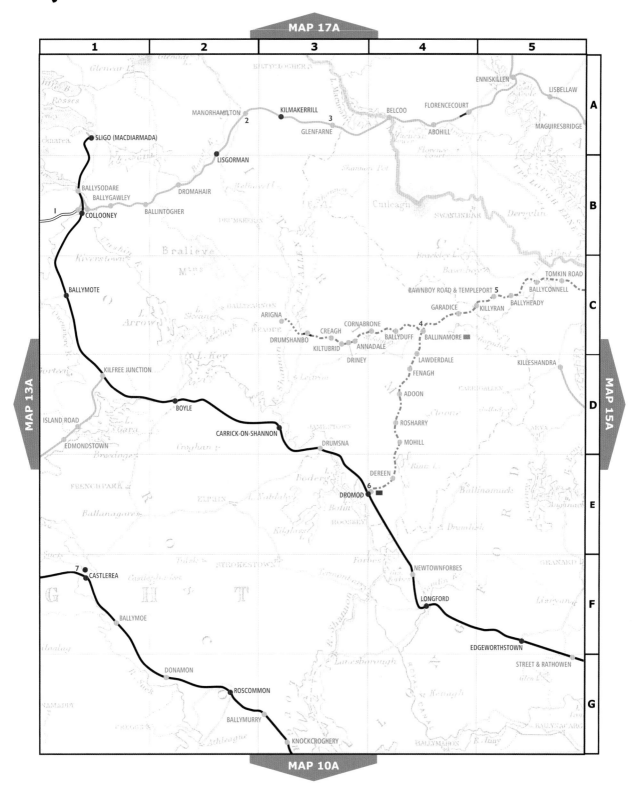

MAP 17A

MAP 13A

MAP 15A

MAP 10A

| | 1 | 2 | 3 | 4 | 5 | |

ENNISKILLEN
LISBELLAW
KILMAKERRILL
MANORHAMILTON 2
BELCOO
FLORENCECOURT
A
GLENFARNE 3
ABOHILL
MAGUIRESBRIDGE
SLIGO (MACDIARMADA)
LISGORMAN
BALLYSODARE
BALLYGAWLEY
DROMAHAIR
B
COLLOONEY
BALLINTOGHER
TOMKIN ROAD
BALLYMOTE
BAWNBOY ROAD & TEMPLEPORT 5
BALLYCONNELL
GARADICE
BALLYHEADY
ARIGNA
KILLYRAN
C
CORNABRONE
CREAGH
4
DRUMSHANBO
BALLYDUFF
BALLINAMORE
KILTUBRID
ANNADALE
KILFREE JUNCTION
DRINEY
LAWDERDALE
KILLESHANDRA
FENAGH
BOYLE
ADOON
ISLAND ROAD
ROSHARRY
CARRICK-ON-SHANNON
EDMONDSTOWN
DRUMSNA
MOHILL
D
DEREEN
DROMOD 6
E
NEWTOWNFORBES
CASTLEREA 7
LONGFORD
BALLYMOE
F
DONAMON
EDGEWORTHSTOWN
ROSCOMMON
STREET & RATHOWEN
BALLYMURRY
G
KNOCKCROGHERY

LEGEND

1 Line mothballed against envisaged reopening as part of the Western Rail Corridor Project
2 MANORHAMILTON: Part of site cleared as a cattle market
3 GLENFARNE: Restored station now a private residence occasionally open to the public ☐ check internet and press for details
4 BALLINAMORE: Site of buildings now part of a school complex
5 BAWNBOY ROAD & TEMPLEPORT: Former station building now the Templeport Resource Centre local amenity
6 DROMOD: Former CLR station building, loco shed and short length of track restored as the 3ft gauge CAVAN & LEITRIM RAILWAY. www.cavanandleitrim.com
7 CASTLEREA RAILWAY MUSEUM adjacent to the Hell's Kitchen public house. www.hellskitchenmuseum.com

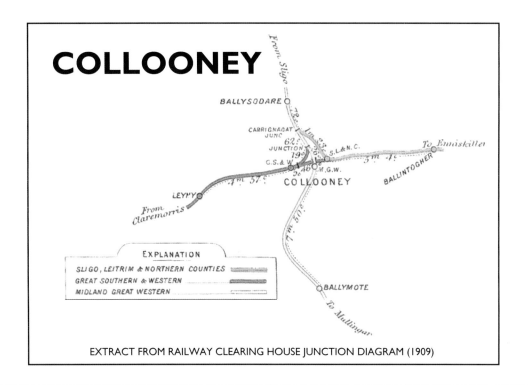

EXTRACT FROM RAILWAY CLEARING HOUSE JUNCTION DIAGRAM (1909)

THE SLIGO, LEITRIM & NORTHERN COUNTIES RAILWAY

For a concern of its size, the Sligo, Leitrim & Northern Counties Railway was most unusual in that it possessed just a single main line and no branches. Authorised by Act of Parliament on 11 August 1875, the one line opened (for passengers) in stages, from 18 March 1879 to 7 November 1882, and ran from Enniskillin – which station it shared with the GNR(I) – to Carrignagat Junction where it met the MGWR, a total distance of 42¾ miles; the company had running powers for the next 4½ miles into the MGWR's Sligo station.

By virtue of the fact that the line, in later years, crossed the border between Northern Ireland and the Free State, it could not be absorbed satisfactorily by a single company or authority, and so retained its independence to the end, eventually closing on 30 September 1957, by which time virtually all passenger services were being operated by diesel railcars.

The station name board on the platform at Sligo in 1998 - though why the addition of 'STATION' was ever deemed necessary is baffling.
Harry Maeers

An anonymous postcard view of a mixed train on the CLR's Arigna Tramway extension. The locomotive is (probably) No.5T, one of four very similar 2-6-2 tank engines built by Hunslet of Leeds for the TDR at the end of the 19th Century and acquired by the CLR between 1941 and 1957.   *K.Turner Collection*

THE CAVAN & LEITRIM RAILWAY

The Cavan, Leitrim & Roscommon Light Railway & Tramway Company limited – to give it its full title – was incorporated in 1883 under the provisions of the Tramways and Public Companies (Ireland) Act of that year and operated a 3ft gauge system composed of one main line and one branch. The main line, 33¾ miles in length, ran in a southwesterly direction from the GNR(I)'s (shared) branch terminus at Belturbet in County Cavan, to their own station next to the MGWR's station at Dromod (in County Leitrim) on its main line to Sligo. This opened on 17 October 1887. A westwards branch of 14¾ miles from Ballinamore, midway along the main line, to Arigna (in County Roscommon), followed on 2 May 1888; known as the Arigna Tramway, this was very much a cheaply laid roadside tramway mirroring the bends and undulations of the highway. The only later addition to the railway came when a 4¼-mile goods extension from Arigna to the local coal workings – coal being a scarce natural resource in Ireland – was opened on 2 June 1920, financed by the Government. Interestingly, the railway was steam-worked until the very end (31 March 1959), by which time it had followed the customary pattern of passing through the hands of the GSR to the CIE. Initially there were eight 4-4-0 tank engines built by Robert Stephenson in 1884, joined twenty years later by a large 0-6-4 tank from the same company. After the 1925 Amalgamation other engines arrived, transfers from the CBPR (four) and the TDR (three). Prior to this, in 1920, two locomotives had been transferred from the NCC for use on the construction, and first year of working, of the Arigna extension.

Dromod station is now the operating base of the new Cavan & Leitrim Railway while two original engines have survived into preservation: No.2 *Kathleen* is at the Ulster Folk & Transport Museum, Cultra and sister engine No.3 *Lady Edith* is in New Jersey, USA.

MAP 15
1 JANUARY 1920

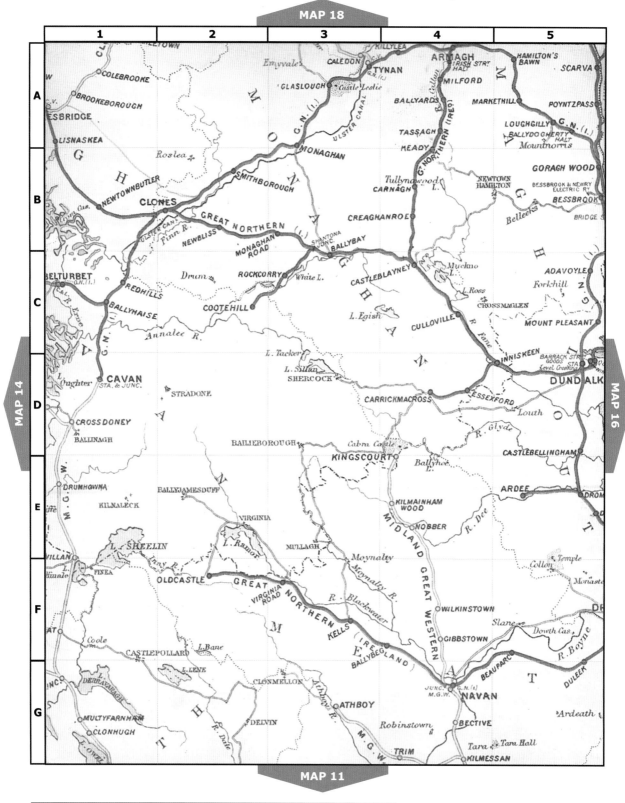

LEGEND

All lines 5ft 3in gauge except:
3ft gauge BESSBROOK & NEWRY TRAMWAY (B5)
3ft gauge CAVAN & LEITRIM RAILWAY (C1)
3ft gauge CLOGHER VALLEY RAILWAY (A1, A3)

A3 TYNAN [GNR(I)]: Full name was TYNAN & CALEDON; originally named TYNAN, CALEDON & MIDDLETOWN and a
    shared station with the CVR's TYNAN terminus
A4 ARMAGH: Full name was ARMAGH RAILWAY STREET
B5 BESSBROOK: Originally named NEWRY
B5 GORAGH WOOD: Correct name was GORAGHWOOD
C1 BALLYHAISE: Originally named BELTURBET JUNCTION
C4 CASTLEBLAYNEY: Originally named CASTLEBLANEY
C5 MOUNT PLEASANT: Originally named PLASTER but closed by this date
D5 DUNDALK: Full name was DUNDALK JUNCTION; originally named DUNDALK
D5 DUNDALK BARRACK STREET: Former passenger station, goods-only
E1 DRUMHOWNA: Also timetabled as DRUMHOWNAGH
E5 DROMIN: Full name was DROMIN JUNCTION
F1 FLOAT: Also timetabled as FLOAT, CASTLEPOLLARD
F4 PROUDSTOWN PARK: A halt existed here for race traffic only. (See MAP 15A)
G1 INNY JUNCTION: Originally named CAVAN JUNCTION

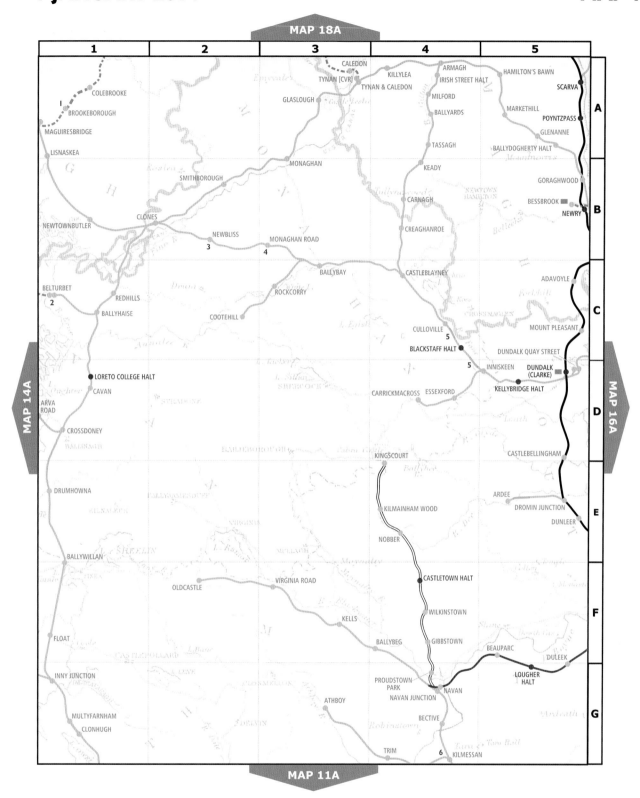

MAP 18A

MAP 11A

MAP 14A

MAP 16A

	1	2	3	4	5

A B C D E F G

CALEDON
TYNAN [CVR]
TYNAN & CALEDON
KILLYLEA
GLASLOUGH
ARMAGH
IRISH STREET HALT
MILFORD
HAMILTON'S BAWN
SCARVA
COLEBROOKE
BROOKEBOROUGH
MAGUIRESBRIDGE
MARKETHILL
POYNTZPASS
GLENANNE
BALLYARDS
LISNASKEA
TASSAGH
BALLYDOGHERTY HALT
MONAGHAN
SMITHBOROUGH
KEADY
GORAGHWOOD
CARNAGH
BESSBROOK
NEWRY
CLONES
NEWTOWNBUTLER
NEWBLISS
MONAGHAN ROAD
CREAGHANROE
BALLYBAY
CASTLEBLAYNEY
ADAVOYLE
BELTURBET
REDHILLS
BALLYHAISE
ROCKCORRY
COOTEHILL
MOUNT PLEASANT
CULLOVILLE
BLACKSTAFF HALT
DUNDALK QUAY STREET
INNISKEEN
DUNDALK (CLARKE)
LORETO COLLEGE HALT
CAVAN
ARVA ROAD
CARRICKMACROSS
ESSEXFORD
KELLYBRIDGE HALT
CROSSDONEY
CASTLEBELLINGHAM
DRUMHOWNA
KINGSCOURT
ARDEE
DROMIN JUNCTION
DUNLEER
KILMAINHAM WOOD
NOBBER
BALLYWILLAN
CASTLETOWN HALT
OLDCASTLE
VIRGINIA ROAD
WILKINSTOWN
FLOAT
KELLS
BALLYBEG
GIBBSTOWN
BEAUPARC
DULEEK
INNY JUNCTION
PROUDSTOWN PARK
NAVAN JUNCTION
NAVAN
LOUGHER HALT
MULTYFARNHAM
CLONHUGH
ATHBOY
BECTIVE
TRIM
KILMESSAN

LEGEND

1 BROOKEBOROUGH: Former station building now a community centre. www.riverbrookeinitiative.com
2 BELTURBET: Former station building now a railway museum; former goods shed now a conference/community centre. www.discoverbelturbet.ie
3 NEWBLISS: Former station building now a picture framing studio/shop. www.darac.ie
4 MONAGHAN ROAD: Former station building now a furniture showroom
5 Parts of the MONAGHAN WAY. www.irishtrails.ie
6 KILMESSAN: Former station building now a hotel. www.stationhousehotel.ie

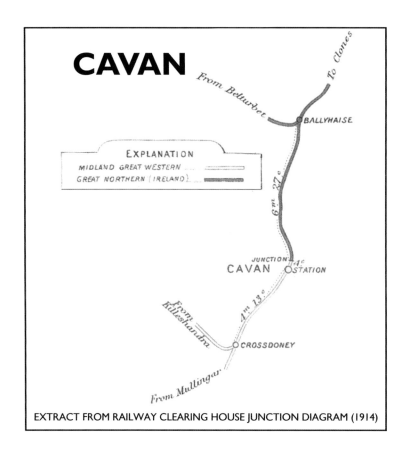

EXTRACT FROM RAILWAY CLEARING HOUSE JUNCTION DIAGRAM (1914)

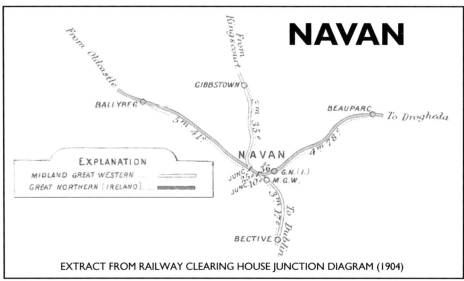

EXTRACT FROM RAILWAY CLEARING HOUSE JUNCTION DIAGRAM (1904)

THE BESSBROOK & NEWRY TRAMWAY

The Bessbrook & Newry Tramway was a 3ft gauge railway, unusual in Ireland in being worked by electricity supplied by a centrally placed third rail. (At a level crossing the current was taken from an overhead wire for safety reasons – the first regular use of such a supply system in the British Isles.) Just over 3 miles in length, it ran from its own platform by the GNR(I) station at Newry out to the flax mill complex at Bessbrook. Incorporated in 1884 under the Tramways and Public Companies (Ireland) Act of the previous year – hence its official title – it opened in October 1885 (exact date unknown) and closed on 10 January 1948.

THE CLOGHER VALLEY RAILWAY

The Clogher Valley Railway, some 37 miles in length, was a 3ft gauge roadside railway serving a sparsely populated region straddling the county boundary between Fermanagh and Tyrone. Constructed under the provisions of the Tramways and Public Companies Act of 1883, it was opened (as the Clogher Valley Tramway) on 2 May 1887 and ran between the GNR(I)'s stations at Tynan in the east and Maguiresbridge in the west; the change of name to its more usually seen title occurred on 16 July 1894. The line closed, in its entirety, on the very last day of 1941.

EXTRACT FROM RAILWAY CLEARING HOUSE JUNCTION DIAGRAM (1907)

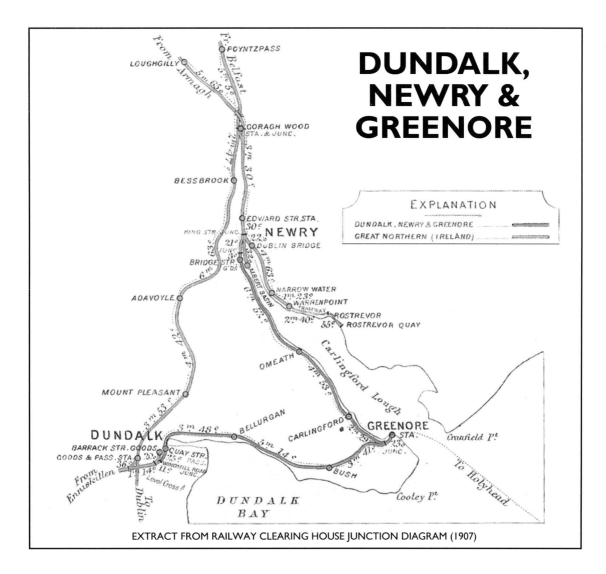

EXTRACT FROM RAILWAY CLEARING HOUSE JUNCTION DIAGRAM (1907)

THE WARRENPOINT & ROSTREVOR TRAMWAY

The Warrenpoint & Rostrevor Tramway was a 3ft gauge single-track horse tramway running more than 3 miles from its own platform at the GNR(I)'s Warrenpoint station along the road beside Carlingford Lough to the smaller resort of Rostrevor, terminating on the quayside there outside the Great Northern Hotel. The line was opened in July 1877 (exact date unknown) by the Warrenpoint & Rostrevor Tramways [sic] Company, incorporated 6 September 1875; it closed in February 1915 after a gale washed away part of the track – though it still appears on the 1920 RGH Map.

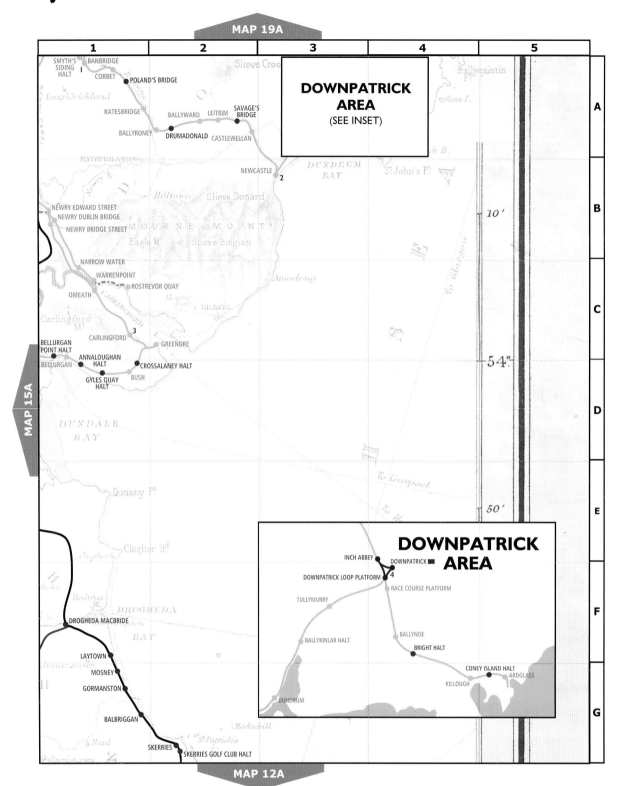

DOWNPATRICK
AREA
(SEE INSET)

DOWNPATRICK
AREA

MAP 12A

MAP 15A

LEGEND

1 BANBRIDGE: Site largely cleared as an Ulsterbus depot, although the
former engine shed remains
2 NEWCASTLE: Former station building now a supermarket
3 CARLINGFORD: Former station building now the Cooley Peninsula
Tourist Office. www.carlingford.ie
4 5ft 3in gauge DOWNPATRICK & COUNTY DOWN RAILWAY.
www.downrail.co.uk

MAP 16

1 JANUARY 1920

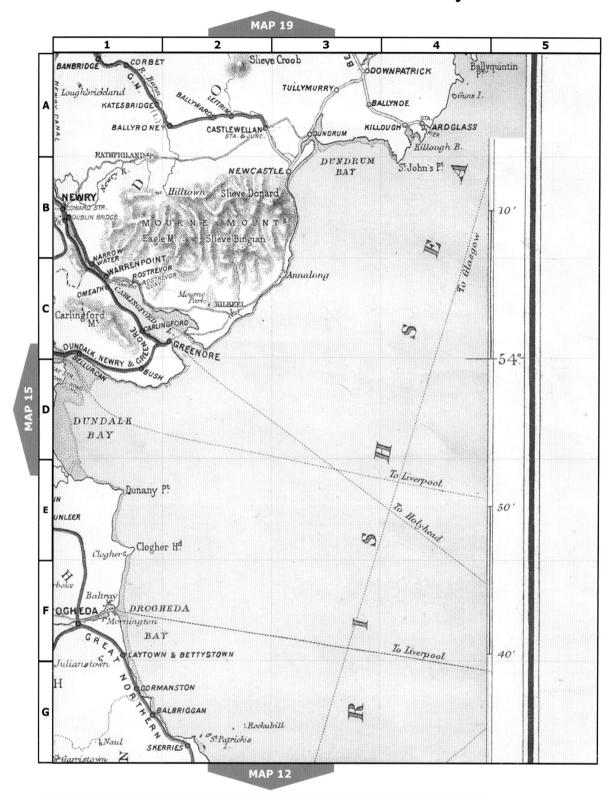

MAP 19

| | 1 | 2 | 3 | 4 | 5 |

BANBRIDGE CORBET
Loughbrickland
KATESBRIDGE
BALLYWARD
BALLYRONEY
CASTLEWELLAN STA. & JUNC.
RATHFRILAND
NEWRY
EDWARD STR.
DUBLIN BRIDGE
Hilltown
NEWCASTLE
Slieve Donard
MOURNE MOUNT^S
Eagle Mt Slieve Bingian
NARROW WATER
WARRENPOINT
ROSTREVOR
ROSTREVOR QUAY
OMEATH
CARLINGFORD
Carlingford M^t
CARLINGFORD L
GREENORE
DUNDALK, NEWRY & GRE...
BELLURCAN
BUSH
Slieve Croob
TULLYMURRY
DUNDRUM
LEITRIM
DOWNPATRICK
BALLYNOE
KILLOUGH
ARDGLASS
Killough B.
St. John's P^t
DUNDRUM BAY
Mourne Park
KILKEEL
Annalong
Ballyquintin P^t
Guns I.
To Glasgow
10'
54°
To Liverpool
To Holyhead
50'
DUNDALK BAY
Dunany P^t
DUNLEER
Clogher H^d
Clogher
Baltray
DROGHEDA
Mornington
DROGHEDA BAY
LAYTOWN & BETTYSTOWN
Julianstown
GORMANSTON
GREAT NORTHERN
BALBRIGGAN
Naul
SKERRIES
Garristown
St. Patrick's I.
Rockabill
To Liverpool
40'
I R I S H S E A

MAP 15

MAP 12

LEGEND

All lines 5ft 3in gauge except:
3ft gauge BESSBROOK & NEWRY TRAMWAY
3ft gauge WARRENPOINT & ROSTREVOR TRAMWAY (C1) – NB Closed by this time

A1 SMYTH'S SIDING HALT: An untimetabled halt existed here north of BANBRIDGE. (See MAP 16A)
A3 BALLYKINLAR HALT, located halfway between TULLMURRY and DUNDRUM, was an unadvertised Army camp halt. (See Map 16A)
A3 DOWNPATRICK RACECOURSE PLATFORM, located south of Ardglass Junction, was an unadvertised halt used only on race days. (See Map 16A
A3 DOWNPATRICK LOOP PLATFORM was an unadvertised halt immediately north of Ardglass Junction (See MAP 16A)
A4 ARDGLASS freight-only pier line disused
C1 BELLURCAN: Correct name was BELLURGAN
F1 LAYTOWN & BETTYSTOWN formerly LAYTOWN
F1 GORMANSTON formerly GORMANSTOWN

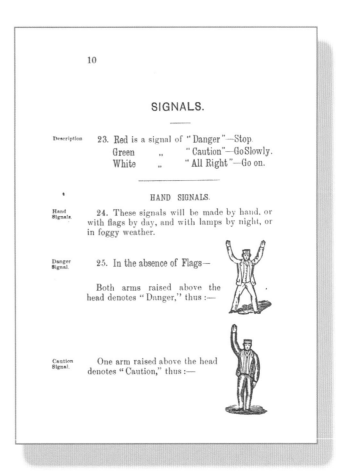

Clogher Valley Tramway Company Limited.

RULES AND REGULATIONS

FOR THE

CONDUCT OF THE TRAFFIC,

AND THE

GUIDANCE OF OFFICERS AND MEN

IN THE

COMPANY'S SERVICE.

BY AUTHORITY OF THE DIRECTORS.

MANCHESTER:
HENRY BLACKLOCK & CO., PRINTERS, ALBERT SQUARE.

10

SIGNALS.

Description 23. Red is a signal of "Danger"—Stop.
            Green   „   "Caution"—Go Slowly.
            White „   "All Right"—Go on.

HAND SIGNALS.

Hand Signals 24. These signals will be made by hand, or with flags by day, and with lamps by night, or in foggy weather.

Danger Signal 25. In the absence of Flags—

Both arms raised above the head denotes "Danger," thus :—

Caution Signal One arm raised above the head denotes "Caution," thus :—

Every railway had – and has – its Rule Book to ensure safe working at all times. The CVR was no exception, as these two sample pages illustrate.

THE GREAT NORTHERN RAILWAY (IRELAND)

The second largest of Ireland's railways, the Great Northern Railway (Ireland), by the time of the 1925 Amalgamation boasted some 617 miles of route, roughly one-third of which covered the region north and west of Dublin and the remainder the region south and west of Belfast in what became Northern Ireland. Indeed, by linking these two cities it had a far greater social and political importance than any other Irish railway. As the GNR(I) it was a relatively late-comer on the scene, being formed in 1876 (on 1 April) though its main constituents – the Ulster Railway and the Dublin & Drogheda Railway (both incorporated in 1836) and the Dublin & Belfast Junction Railway (1845) were considerably older. The main line between Dublin and Belfast was finally completed on 5 April 1855 with the opening of a bridge over the River Boyne in Drogheda. A host of other company absorptions and branch line additions, as well as a main line from Belfast to Londonderry, completed the system.

The complicated cross-border nature of the many of its lines helped the GNR(I) retain its independence following the political partition of Ireland, though financial difficulties after World War II resulted in the formation of the Great Northern Railway Board, backed by both governments, to buy and operate the railway; this it did as from 1 September 1953. Five years later, on 1 October 1958, the Board was dissolved and the railway's assets divided between the UTA and the CIE – with wholesale closures commencing until only today's skeleton of the system remains.

During its lifetime the GNR(I) inherited, bought or built at its Dundalk Works a total of nearly 400 locomotives, of which four survive in varying states of preservation: No.93 (JT Class 2-4-2 tank of 1895), is at the Ulster Folk & Transport Museum, Cultra, whilst the RPSI's base at Whitehead is home to No.85 *Merlin* (V Class 4-4-0 of 1932), No.131 (Q Class 4-4-0 of 1901) and No.171 *Slieve Gullion* (S Class 4-4-0 of 1932). Cultra is also home to railbus No.1, an AEC motor bus of 1929 vintage converted by the GNR(I) in 1932.

THE BELFAST & COUNTY DOWN RAILWAY

With 80 miles of routes – all within County Down – the BCDR was a compact little system that comprehensively covered the region to the south and east of Belfast. The first of its lines, authorised by Act of Parliament on 20 January 1846, ran from Belfast Queen's Quay to Holywood on the southern shore of Belfast Lough; this opened on 2 August 1848 and was followed by a second line from Belfast to Newtownards via Comber (1850), then a continuation of what became the main line from Comber southwards to Ballynahinch (1858) then Downpatrick (1859, isolating Ballynahinch at the end of a short branch); two years later a northern branch from Comber to the coast at Donaghadee was opened. Later extensions to the system by other companies were worked and/or absorbed by the BCDR; these served Bangor to the north (1865), and Newcastle (1869), Ardglass (1892) and Castlewellan (1906) to the south. In 1948 the railway was taken over by the UTA – and the closures began (whilst diesel units replaced steam working). All that remains today is the busy commuter line to Bangor.

The BCDR has been comparatively very well served by the Irish railway preservation movement. Downpatrick is now the operating base for the 4-mile-long Downpatrick & County Down Railway – Ireland's only preserved standard gauge line – and home to several items of BCDR rolling-stock whilst ex-BCDR No.30, a 4-4-2 tank engine built by Beyer, Peacock in 1901, is housed in the Ulster Folk & Transport Museum, Cultra.

THE DUNDALK, NEWRY & GREENORE RAILWAY

The history of the Dundalk, Newry & Greenore Railway has always been inextricably linked with that of the Irish Sea ferries operated by the LNWR and its successor the LMS. It began life as the Dundalk & Greenore Railway, a short line between Dundalk and the port of Greenore authorised by an Act of Parliament on 28 July 1863 and financed by the LNWR. The railway opened on 30 April 1873, with steamer services to Holyhead commencing at the beginning of May. An Act of Parliament of 21 July that same year authorised the DGR, with a change of name to the DNGR, to construct the second half of its system: a line from Greenore northwards along the western side of Carlingford Lough to Newry. This opened on 1 August 1876, with a connection made from the DNGR's Bridge Street station to that of the GNR(I) at Edward Street. Total length of the two routes was 26½ miles. With the 1923 Grouping of the railways in Great Britain the DNGR passed, with the LNWR, into the remit of the LMS while from 1 July 1933 the railway was worked by the GNR(I). Following the 1948 Nationalisation of British railways, control passed to the British Transport Commission – who closed it on the last day of 1951.

Motive power was originally in the form of six Crewe-built 0-6-0 saddle tanks; these were augmented in GNR(I) days by that company's JT Class 2-4-2 tanks for passenger workings. One of the 2-4-2 tanks, No.93 of 1895, is preserved at the Ulster Folk & Transport Museum, Cultra, along with an original DNGR 6-wheeler carriage.

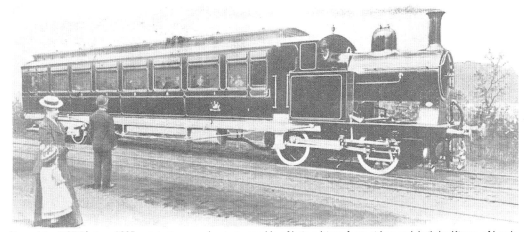

One of the BCDR's two 1905 autotrains or railmotors, capable of being driven from either end, built by Kitson of Leeds. (A third was supplied a year later.) They were used from 1905 – the year this postcard was sent – to work an intensive shuttle service between Belfast and Holywood until 1918, after which the power units were scrapped and the carriage portions converted into auto-trailers.   *K.Turner Collection*

MAP 17

1 JANUARY 1920

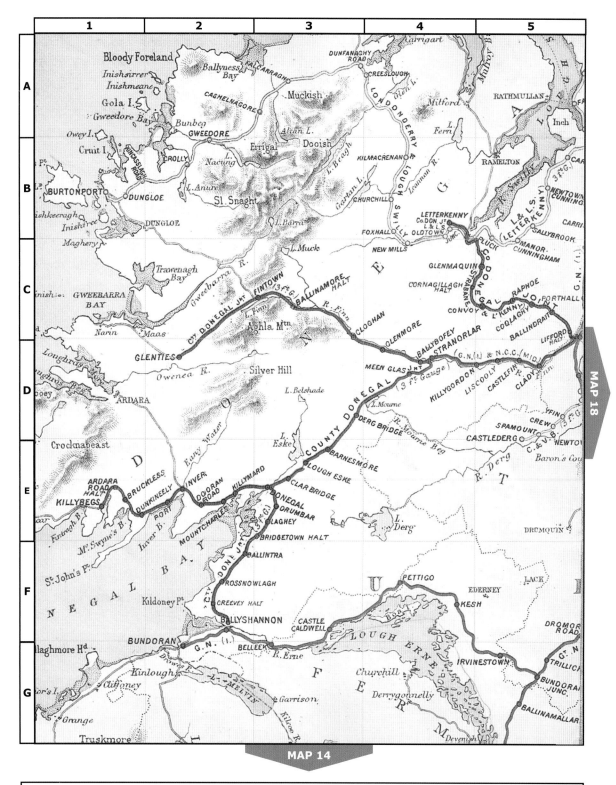

LEGEND

MAP 18

MAP 14

All lines 3ft gauge except:
5ft 3in gauge GREAT NORTHERN RAILWAY (F2 – F4, G2 – G5,)

A5 GOLF HALT: A golf club platform existed between BUNCRANA and FAHAN (See MAP 17A)
B1 DUNGLOE: Originally named LOUGHMEALA
B5 MANORCUNNINGHAM: Originally named MANOR CUNNINGHAM;
    also timetabled as MANOR
B5 NEWTOWNCUNNINGHAM: Correct name was NEWTONCUNNINGHAM;
    originally named NEWTOWNCUNNINGHAM (also NEWTOWN CUNNINGHAM).
    Also timetabled as NEWTON
C2 SHALLOGANS HALT: A halt existed here 3 miles north of GLENTIES
C3 BALLINAMORE HALT: Correct name was BALLINAMORE
C5 COOLAGHY: Full name was COOLAGHY HALT
D3 DERG BRIDGE: Full name was DERG BRIDGE HALT
D4 MEEN GLAS: Correct name was MEENGLAS HALT; station was closed c1918 – c1936
D5 CASTLEFIN: correct name was CASTLEFINN
    though also known (and signed) as CASTLEFIN

D5 LISCOOLY: Originally named LISCOOLEY
E1 ARDARA ROAD HALT: Originally named ARDARA ROAD
E2 DOORAN ROAD: Correct name was DOORIN ROAD
E2 KILLYMARD: Full name was KILLYMARD HALT
E2 PORT HALT: Originally named PORT
E3 BARNESMORE: Full name was BARNESMORE HALT;
    originally named BARRACK BRIDGE HALT
E3 CLAR BRIDGE: Full name was CLAR BRIDGE HALT
E3 DRUMBAR: Full name was DRUMBAR HALT
E3 HOSPITAL HALT: An untimetabled halt existed ½ mile south of DONEGAL
E3 LOUGH ESKE: Originally named DRUMININ
F2 CREEVEY HALT: Correct name was CREEVY HALT
F3 CASTLE CALDWELL: Correct name was CASTLECALDWELL
G5 BUNDORAN JUNCTION: Originally named LOWTHERSTOWN ROAD

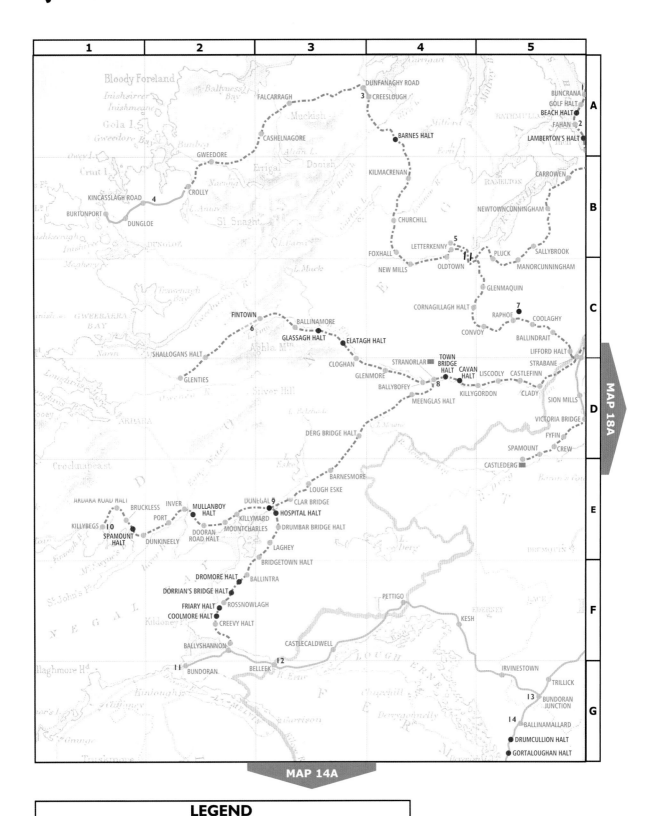

MAP 18A

MAP 14A

LEGEND

1 BUNCRANA: Former station building now a bar and restaurant. www.thedriftinn.ie
2 FAHAN: Former station building now a restaurant. www.fireboxgrill.com
3 Part of the MUCKISH RAILWAY LOOP WALK
4 BURTONPORT OLD RAILWAY WALK
5 LETTERKENNY [CDRJC]: Site largely cleared as a bus station
6 FINTOWN RAILWAY. www.antraen.com
7 OAKFIELD PARK: Home to a 15in gauge 2½-mile miniature railway. www.oakfieldpark.com
8 STRANORLAR: Site cleared as a bus depot with a new clock tower incorporating the former station clock
9 DONEGAL: Now the DONEGAL RAILWAY HERITAGE CENTRE
10 KILLYBEGS: Site now under a road
11 BUNDORAN: Site cleared as a car park
12 BELLEEK: Former station building now the Steppings Stones childcare centre
13 BUNDORAN JUNCTION: Former signal cabin undergoing restoration at the DOWNPATRICK & COUNTY DOWN RAILWAY (see MAP 16A)
14 BALLINMALLARD: Former station building now the Rascals Playstation childcare centre

LETTERKENNY & STRABANE

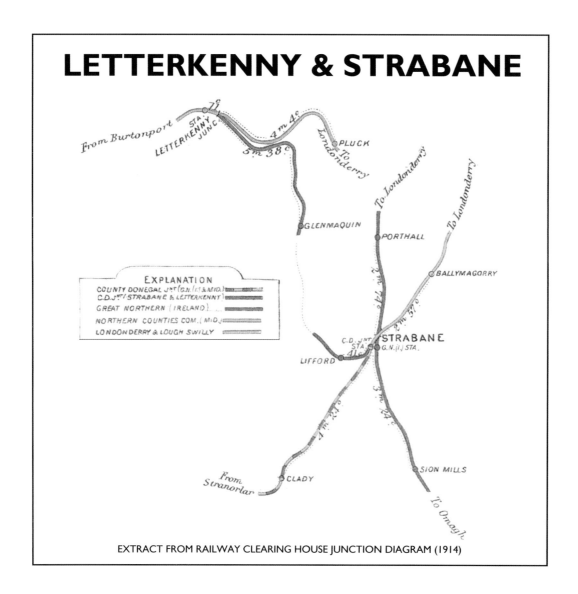

EXTRACT FROM RAILWAY CLEARING HOUSE JUNCTION DIAGRAM (1914)

THE NCC STANDARD GAUGE

The Belfast-based Midland Railway, Northern Counties Committee – to give it its full title – was an off-shoot of the British Midland Railway which, on 1 July 1903, took over the Belfast & Northern Counties Railway. The BNCR had begun life as the Belfast & Ballymena Railway, incorporated on 21 July 1845 by Act of Parliament and opened between those two places on 11 April 1848 (with short branches to Carrickfergus and Randalstown). The change of name came in 1860, after which the company set about taking over neighbouring railways until by 1903 it covered a whole swathe of north-east Ireland from Belfast and Larne in the east to Londonderry and Strabane in the west. By the time of the British 1923 Grouping, when the NCC became part of the LMS NCC, it was Ireland's fourth largest railway with 201 miles of standard gauge routes plus 64 miles of narrow gauge lines (see later pages).

On 1 January 1948 the railway was nationalised as the Railway Executive, Northern Counties Committee; a year later, on 1 April 1949, it was bought by the UTA. Today only the main lines to Londonderry and Larne Harbour, and the short branch to Portrush, remain open. Two locomotives from the motley BNCRstock of inherited, bought and built engines have survived into preservation: No.4, a 1947 WT Class 2-6-4 tank, which is with the RPSI at Whitehead and No.74 *Dunluce Castle*, a U2 Class 4-4-0 of 1924 vintage, now at the Ulster Folk & Transport Museum, Cultra.

CASTLEDERG & VICTORIA BRIDGE TRAMWAY

The Castlederg & Victoria Bridge Tramway was a 3ft gauge roadside steam tramway, operated by the Castlederg & Victoria Bridge Tramway Company (incorporated 16 July 1883), linking the two small towns of its title – a distance of just over 7 miles. Authorised by the Castlederg and Victoria Bridge Tramway Act of 1883, it opened on 11 July 1884 and closed never to reopen, on 31 January 1933, when the staff joined a Northern Ireland railway strike. (The official closure date was 3 October that year.) There were three official intermediate halts between the grand Castlederg terminus – complete with two market goods spurs – and its own platform by the GNR(I)'s Victoria Bridge station ,though in practice trains would stop anywhere when requested to.

THE CDRJC

The County Donegal Railways Joint Committee controlled a large system of 3ft gauge lines in north-west Ireland. Its roots lay in the 13½-mile standard gauge Finn Railway, opened on 7 September 1863 between Strabane and Stranorlar, and the 18-mile 3ft gauge West Donegal Railway opened in stages between 25 April 1882 and 16 September 1889 from Stranorlar on to Donegal. The two ventures amalgamated in 1892 as the Donegal Railway and the decision taken to convert the Finn Railway to the narrower gauge.

Four extensions followed: a 19-mile branch from Donegal to Killybegs (1893), a 24-mile branch from Stranorlar to Glenties (1895), a 14½-mile extension from Strabane back to Londonderry (1900) and a 15½mile branch from Donegal to Ballyshannon (1905). Then, on 1 May 1906, the Midland Railway of Britain and the GNR(I) agreed to take over the railway, changing its name to the County Donegal Railways Joint Committee. The final addition to the system came in 1909 with the opening of the nominally independent 19-mile Strabane & Londonderry Railway, owned by the MR but worked as part of the whole. Financial pressures after World War II saw the closure of the Glenties branch to passengers on 3 December 1947 (and to goods on 12 March 1952) and then the entire remainder of the railway on 31 December 1959 (though some goods workings continued for another month or so), leaving the whole of County Donegal rail-free.

The CDRJC possessed 23 locomotives in all, all narrow gauge tank engines (the Finn Railway being worked with borrowed engines) of which four survive, all 2-6-4 Naysmith, Wilson of Lancashire products: No.2 *Blanche* (of 1912, now at the Ulster Folk & Transport Museum, Cultra), No.4 *Meenglas* (of 1902, now at the Foyle Valley Railway), No.5 *Drumboe* (of 1907, undergoing restoration with the RPSI at Whitehead) and No.6 *Columbkille* (also 1907 and also at the Foyle Valley Railway). The CDRJC was also famous for its very mixed fleet of railcars and trailers which, in the final years, were used for almost all passenger workings. At least nine still exist, in various states of completeness, at Cultra, the Donegal Heritage Centre, the Foyle Valley Railway, the Fintown Railway and on the Isle of Man Railway.

THE LONDONDERRY & LOUGH SWILLY RAILWAY

The 99-mile, 3ft gauge Londonderry & Lough Swilly Railway system – the major part of which was in County Donegal – was formed of two lines: one north from Londonderry via Buncrana to Carndonagh and one west from Londonderry via Letterkenny to Burtonport. After a false start with the opening on the last day of 1863 of a short standard gauge section out of Londonderry, and an extension to Buncrana the following year, the decision was taken to convert to narrow gauge as the system began to grow with extensions added by other companies (and taken over or worked by the LLSR). The first section to close, on 30 November 1935, was the Buncrana to Carndonagh extension (opened 1 July 1901); the last was the remainder of the Buncrana line on 8 August 1953 (by then worked by excursion trains only).

During its lifetime the LLSR possessed a total of 28 locomotives from a number of different builders – all tank engines, of which 22 were narrow gauge (including a pair of massive 4-8-4s, the only locomotives of this wheel arrangement to work in the British Isles). Sadly, none survive, though the 'Swilly' name and heritage lives on in the shape of the bus services still run by the company. At one time it operated pleasure steamers on Lough Swilly as well.

MAP 18

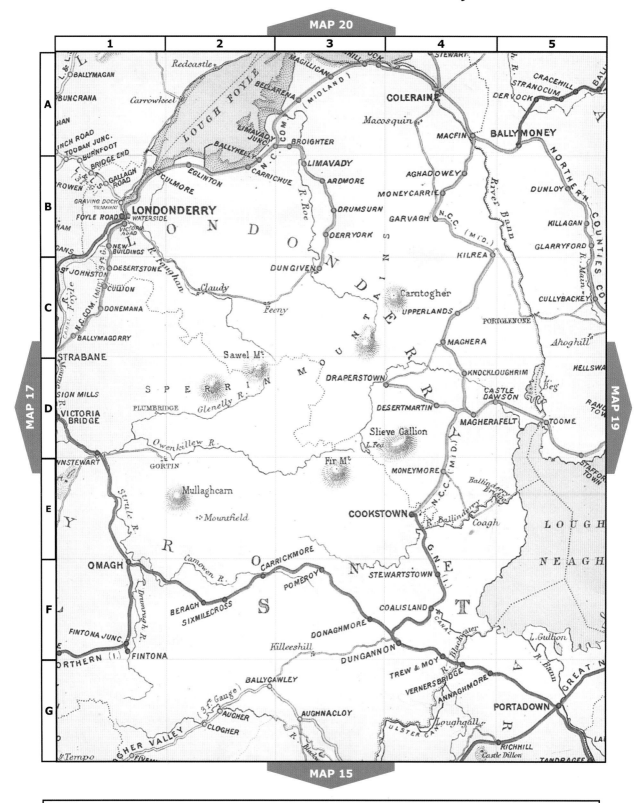

LEGEND

All lines 5ft 3in gauge except:
3ft gauge BALLYCASTLE RAILWAY (A5)
3ft gauge LONDONDERRY & LOUGH SWILLY RAILWAY (A1 – B1)
3ft gauge COUNTY DONEGAL RAILWAYS (B1 – C1)
3ft gauge CLOGHER VALLEY RAILWAY (G1 – G3)
3ft and 5ft 3in mixed-gauge LONDONDERRY quayside tramway (B1)

A3 LIMAVADY JUNCTION: Originally named JUNCTION
A4 COLERAINE: Originally named COLERAINE (NORTHBROOK)
A4 PORT STEWART should be PORTSTEWART
A5 BALLYMONEY: Station shared by the BR and the NCC
A5 CRACEHILL: Correct name was GRACEHILL
B1 TOOBAN JUNCTION: Originally known (variously) as THE JUNCTION, LETTERKENNY JUNCTION and BURNSFOOT JUNCTION
B2 CARRICHUE: Originally named CARRICKHUGH

B4 CURRAGH BRIDGE HALT: A halt existed here midway between AGHADOWEY and MACFIN. (See MAP 18A)
B4 MONEYCARRIE: Full name was MONEYCARRIE HALT
C1 BALLYHEATHER HALT: A request halt existed here midway between BALLYMAGORRY and DONEMANA. (See MAP 18A)
C1 DESERTSTONE: Correct name was DESERTONE HALT
C4 TAMLAGHT HALT: A halt existed here midway between UPPERLANDS and KILREA. (See MAP 18A)
D4 CASTLE DAWSON: Correct name was CASTLEDAWSON
D5 TOOME: Also timetabled as TOOME BRIDGE
E4 KILLYMOON GOLF LINKS: An untimetabled halt existed here, dates unknown. (See MAP 18A)
G4 VERNERSBRIDGE: Originally named VERNER
G5 TANDRAGEE: Correct name was TANDERAGEE; originally named MADDEN BRIDGE

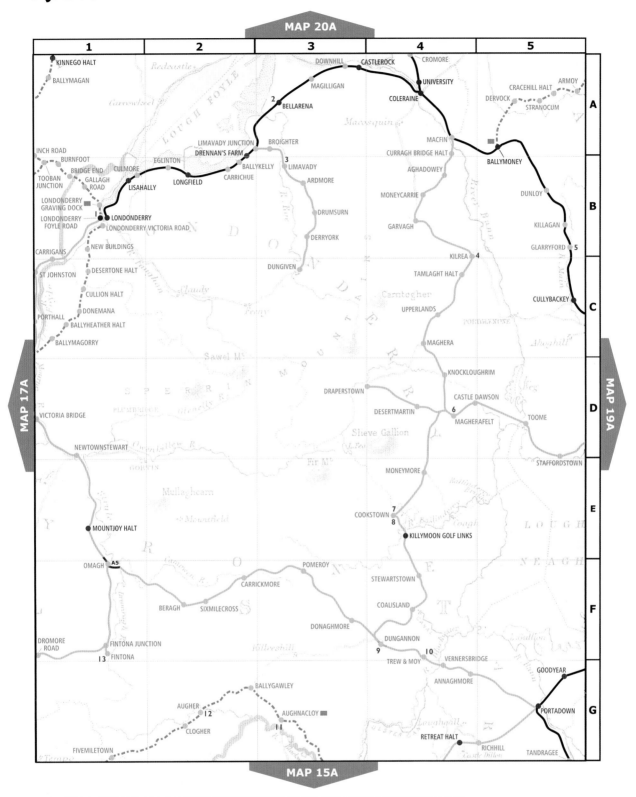

MAP 20A

MAP 17A

MAP 19A

MAP 15A

| | 1 | 2 | 3 | 4 | 5 |

KINNEGO HALT
BALLYMAGAN
DOWNHILL
CASTLEROCK
CROMORE
MAGILLIGAN
UNIVERSITY
CRACEHILL HALT ARMOY
2 BELLARENA
COLERAINE
DERVOCK
STRANOCUM
A

LIMAVADY JUNCTION
BROIGHTER
MACFIN
INCH ROAD
BURNFOOT
DRENNAN'S FARM
CURRAGH BRIDGE HALT
BRIDGE END
EGLINTON
BALLYKELLY
3 LIMAVADY
AGHADOWEY
BALLYMONEY
TOOBAN JUNCTION
GALLAGH ROAD
CULMORE
CARRICHUE
ARDMORE
DUNLOY
B
LISAHALLY
LONGFIELD
MONEYCARRIE
LONDONDERRY GRAVING DOCK
KILLAGAN
LONDONDERRY FOYLE ROAD
1 LONDONDERRY
DRUMSURN
GARVAGH
GLARRYFORD 5
LONDONDERRY VICTORIA ROAD
DERRYORK
CARRIGANS
NEW BUILDINGS
KILREA 4
ST JOHNSTON
DESERTONE HALT
DUNGIVEN
TAMLAGHT HALT
CULLYBACKEY
C
CULLION HALT
PORTHALL
DONEMANA
UPPERLANDS
BALLYHEATHER HALT
BALLYMAGORRY
MAGHERA

KNOCKLOUGHRIM
VICTORIA BRIDGE
DRAPERSTOWN
CASTLE DAWSON
D
DESERTMARTIN
6 MAGHERAFELT
TOOME
NEWTOWNSTEWART
STAFFORDSTOWN

MONEYMORE
MOUNTJOY HALT
7 COOKSTOWN
E
8 KILLYMOON GOLF LINKS

OMAGH A5
POMEROY
STEWARTSTOWN
CARRICKMORE
COALISLAND
F
BERAGH SIXMILECROSS
DONAGHMORE
DUNGANNON
DROMORE ROAD
FINTONA JUNCTION
9 10 TREW & MOY
VERNERSBRIDGE
13 FINTONA
ANNAGHMORE
GOODYEAR

BALLYGAWLEY
AUGHER
12
AUGHNACLOY
PORTADOWN
G
CLOGHER
11
RETREAT HALT
RICHHILL
FIVEMILETOWN
TANDRAGEE

LEGEND

1 LONDONDERRY FOYLE ROAD: Now the FOYLE VALLEY RAILWAY MUSEUM. www.discovernorthernireland.com
2 BELLARENA: Former station building and station master's house now holiday accommodation. www.bellarenarailwaystation.com
3 LIMAVADY: Site now occupied by a bus station
4 KILREA: Former signal box preserved at Garvagh Museum, Garvagh House. www.garvaghmuseum.com
5 GLARRYFORD: Former station building now Glarryford Young Farmers Hall
6 MAGHERAFELT: Now a Department for Regional Development Road Service depot
7 COOKSTOWN [NCC]: Now a Chinese restaurant
8 COOKSTOWN [GNR(I)]: Now Cookstown Hockey Club clubhouse
9 DUNGANNON: Former trackbed through station now a linear park
10 TREW & MOY: Now home to a mushroom distribution business
11 AUGHNACLOY: Former station building now a nursery school
12 AUGHER: Former station building now a restaurant/coffee shop. www.augherstationhouse.co.uk
13 FINTONA: Site largely cleared as a car park

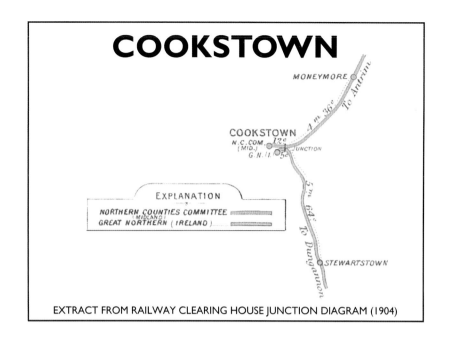

EXTRACT FROM RAILWAY CLEARING HOUSE JUNCTION DIAGRAM (1904)

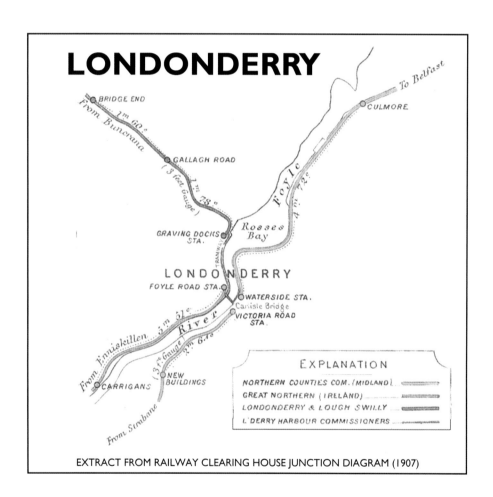

EXTRACT FROM RAILWAY CLEARING HOUSE JUNCTION DIAGRAM (1907)

THE LONDONDERRY QUAYSIDE TRAMWAY

The west bank of the River Foyle was home to a short 3ft/5ft 3in mixed-gauge tramway, owned by the Londonderry Port & Harbour Commissioners, which allowed transfer of goods wagons (and – illegally – passenger trains) between the Graving Dock and Foyle Road stations. Similar mixed-gauge tracks on the lower level of Carlisle Bridge (now Craigavon Bridge) by Foyle Road station allowed wagons to be winched across the river to the Waterside and Victoria Road stations on the east bank. The system fell into disuse following the closure of the Graving Dock (1953) and Foyle Road (1954) stations; the bridge rails were removed in 1967.

The harbour at Coleraine, on the east bank of the River Bann, with the bridge carrying the NCC line to Londonderry in the distance on the extreme right. Less than ½ mile in length, this goods-only harbour branch fell out of use in the 1960s. The small coaster being loaded or unloaded is the Hull-registered *Hawthorn* – small vessels such as these were once a common sight in ports and harbours all around the British Isles, transporting bulky cargoes between them whenever and wherever required. *K.Turner Collection*

THE FINTONA BRANCH

The ¾-mile Fintona branch of the GNR(I) was unique in Ireland in that, from 16 January 1854 until closure on 30 September 1957, passenger services were worked by a double-deck horse-drawn carriage. (Between 15 June 1853 and 16 January 1854 the branch had been the terminal section of the main line from Londonderry of the – then incomplete – Londonderry & Enniskillen Railway before it was bypassed at what became Fintona Junction.)

Goods trains to Fintona were always steam hauled, in conventional fashion, with this traffic ceasing at the same time as the passenger service as part of the region's widespread line closures.

The Fintona branch's second (and last) passenger car, numbered 381 in the GNR(I)'s carriage fleet, was a double-deck tramcar built in 1883 by the Metropolitan Railway Carriage & Wagon Company of Birmingham. It is seen here, outside Fintona station (and shed) in the GNR(I)'s painted teak livery it carried between 1929 and 1946. 1st and 2nd class accommodation was provided in the lower deck saloons; 3rd class passengers rode on the roof. The car is now preserved in the Ulster Folk & Transport Museum, Cultra. The branch's one horse - of whichever sex - was always named Dick.
K.Turner Collection

MAP 19

1 JANUARY 1920

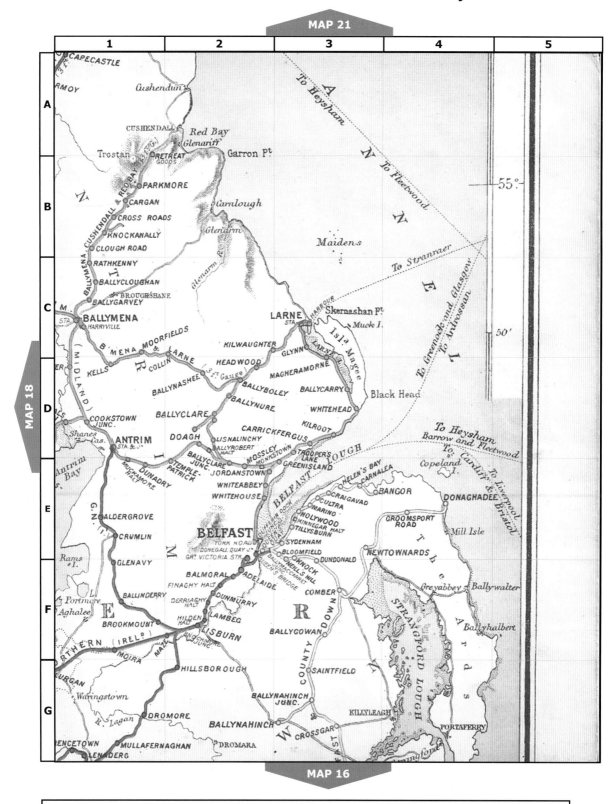

MAP 21

MAP 18

MAP 16

LEGEND

All lines 5ft 3in gauge except:
3ft gauge BALLYCASTLE RAILWAY (A1)
3ft gauge BALLYMENA narrow gauge lines (B1, C1–C3, D1–D2)

B1 RETREAT: Although sometimes timetabled, this was never a passenger station, the line from PARKMORE being goods-only
C1 HARRYVILLE: A goods-only station by this time
C3 KILWAUGHTER: Full name was KILWAUGHTER HALT
C3 MAGHERAMORNE: Originally named BALLYLIG
D1 COOKSTOWN JUNCTION: Originally named DRUMSOUGH
D1 RANDALSTOWN CAMP PLATFORM: An untimetabled military camp halt existed ½ mile west of RANDALSTOWN, exact dates unknown
D2 BALLYBOLEY: Originally named BALLYCLARE JUNCTION; also known as BALLYBOLEY JUNCTION
D2 BALLYEASTON HALT: Originally named BALLYEASTON BRIDGE, a halt existed midway between BALLYNASHEE and BALLYBOLEY
D2 COLLIN: Full name was COLLIN HALT

D2 HEADWOOD: Originally named BALLYGOWAN
E2 BALLYCLARE JUNCTION: Originally named BALLYNURE ROAD
E2 BELFAST GREAT VICTORIA STREET: Originally named BELFAST
E2 BELFAST QUEEN'S BRIDGE: Station closed 1885
E2 MONKSTOWN: Full name was MONKSTOWN HALT
E2 YORK ROAD: Originally named BELFAST YORK ROAD
E3 Halts existed at BALLYMACARRETT and VICTORIA PARK between BELFAST QUEEN'S QUAY and SYDENHAM. (See MAP 19A Inset)
E3 GREENISLAND: Originally named CARRICKFERGUS JUNCTION
E3 HELEN'S BAY: Originally named CLANDEBOYE
E3 KINNEGAR HALT: Originally named KINNEGAR CROSSING HALT
E3 KNOCK: Also timetabled as KNOCK & BELMONT
E3 TILLYSBURN: Full name was TILLYSBURN HALT
E4 GROOMSPORT ROAD: Originally named GROOMSPORT & BANGOR
F2 ADELAIDE: Full name was ADELAIDE & WINDSOR
F2 MAZE: Originally named MAZE PLATFORM

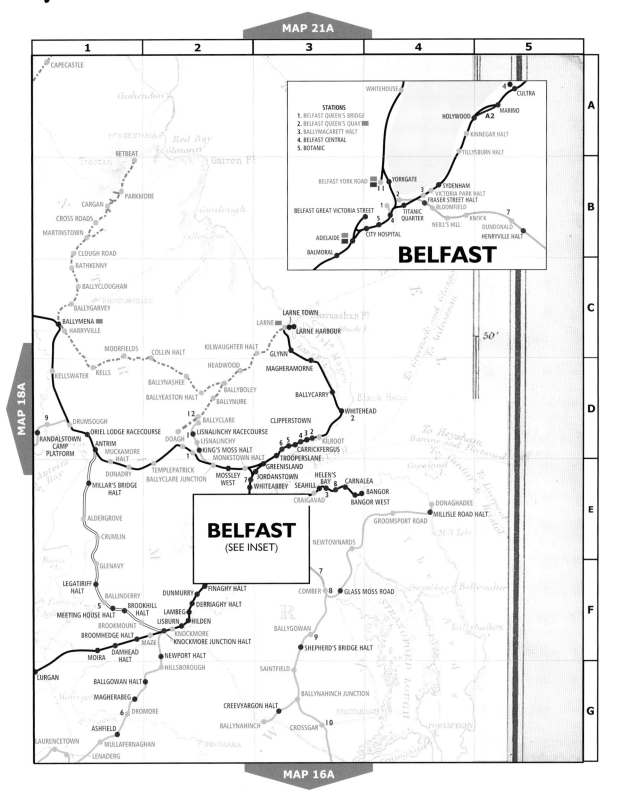

MAP 21A

MAP 18A

MAP 16A

| | 1 | 2 | 3 | 4 | 5 |

CAPECASTLE

RETREAT

PARKMORE
CARGAN
CROSS ROADS
MARTINSTOWN
CLOUGH ROAD
RATHKENNY
BALLYCLOUGHAN
BALLYGARVEY
BALLYMENA
HARRYVILLE
MOORFIELDS
KELLSWATER
KELLS
COLLIN HALT
KILWAUGHTER HALT
HEADWOOD
BALLYNASHEE
BALLYEASTON HALT
BALLYNURE
BALLYBOLEY

LARNE TOWN
LARNE
LARNE HARBOUR
GLYNN
MAGHERAMORNE
BALLYCARRY

DRUMSOUGH
9
ORIEL LODGE RACECOURSE
RANDALSTOWN CAMP PLATFORM
ANTRIM
MUCKAMORE HALT
DUNADRY
TEMPLEPATRICK
BALLYCLARE JUNCTION
DOAGH
12
BALLYCLARE
LISNALINCHY RACECOURSE
LISNALINCHY
KING'S MOSS HALT
MONKSTOWN HALT
CLIPPERSTOWN
KILROOT
CARRICKFERGUS
TROOPERSLANE
GREENISLAND
JORDANSTOWN
MOSSLEY WEST
WHITEABBEY
SEAHILL
CRAIGAVAD
HELEN'S BAY
CARNALEA
BANGOR
BANGOR WEST
WHITEHEAD
2

MILLAR'S BRIDGE HALT
ALDERGROVE
CRUMLIN
GLENAVY
LEGATIRIFF HALT
BALLINDERRY
BROOKHILL HALT
MEETING HOUSE HALT
5
BROOKMOUNT
BROOMHEDGE HALT
MAZE
DAMHEAD HALT
MOIRA
LURGAN
DUNMURRY
FINAGHY HALT
DERRIAGHY HALT
LAMBEG
LISBURN
HILDEN
KNOCKMORE
KNOCKMORE JUNCTION HALT
NEWPORT HALT
HILLSBOROUGH
BALLGOWAN HALT
MAGHERABEG
DROMORE
6
ASHFIELD
MULLAFERNAGHAN
LENADERG
LAURENCETOWN

BELFAST
(SEE INSET)

NEWTOWNARDS
COMBER
8
GLASS MOSS ROAD
GROOMSPORT ROAD
DONAGHADEE
MILLISLE ROAD HALT
BALLYGOWAN
9
SHEPHERD'S BRIDGE HALT
SAINTFIELD
BALLYNAHINCH JUNCTION
CREEVYARGON HALT
BALLYNAHINCH
CROSSGAR
10
7

BELFAST (inset)

STATIONS
1. BELFAST QUEEN'S BRIDGE
2. BELFAST QUEEN'S QUAY
3. BALLYMACARETT HALT
4. BELFAST CENTRAL
5. BOTANIC

WHITEHOUSE
CULTRA
4
MARINO
HOLYWOOD
A2
KINNEGAR HALT
TILLYSBURN HALT
BELFAST YORK ROAD
11
YORKGATE
SYDENHAM
VICTORIA PARK HALT
FRASER STREET HALT
BLOOMFIELD
2
3
BELFAST GREAT VICTORIA STREET
1
TITANIC QUARTER
4
5
NEILL'S HILL
KNOCK
DUNDONALD
HENRYVILLE HALT
7
ADELAIDE
CITY HOSPITAL
BALMORAL

50'

STATIONS
1. BALLYROBERT HALT
2. EDEN HALT
3. DOWNSHIRE
4. BARN HALT
5. CLIPPERSTOWN
6. MOUNT HALT
7. BLEACH GREEN HALT
8. CRAWFORDSBURN
9. RANDALSTOWN

BELFAST

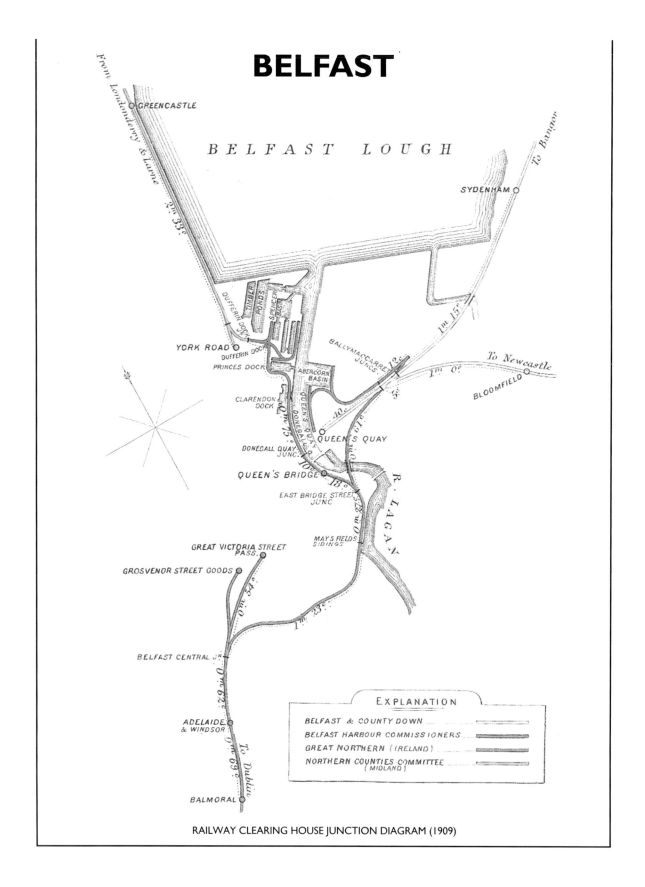

RAILWAY CLEARING HOUSE JUNCTION DIAGRAM (1909)

NCC N Class 0-4-0 saddle tank No.16 used for shunting at York Road, Belfast captured before its 1951 withdrawal. The only member of its class, No.6 was built in the city in 1914. *K.Turner Collection*

THE BALLYMENA NARROW GAUGE

Two 3ft gauge railways ran north and south from the Antrim town of Ballymena: the Ballymena, Cushendall & Red Bay Railway (incorporated by Act of Parliament on 18 July 1872) and the Ballymena & Larne Railway (incorporated by Act of Parliament on 7 August 1874) respectively. The first opened in stages, from 26 May 1875, with a number of short goods-only branches off its single line indicating the reliance the railway placed on coal and mineral traffic. Indeed, passenger services did not commence until 5 April 1886. The 16½-mile line was worked with just three 0-4-2 saddle tanks built in 1874 by Black, Hawthorn of Gateshead.

The BLR had a 25¼-mile main line running between Ballymena and Larne Harbour, plus a 4¾-mile branch to Doagh. It too opened in stages: for goods on 1 August 1877 and for passengers from 24 April the following year. Working was with six Beyer, Peacock tank engines of various designs, supplied between 1877 and 1880. Increasingly poor financial positions led to both lines being taken over, in 1903 and 1923 respectively, by the NCC, which body added six more tank engines to the lines' stock. (A physical connection in Ballymena allowed for through running of freight trains.) Passenger services ceased from 1 October 1930 over the former BCRBR and from Ballyclare to Doagh on the former BLR; the remaining services were ended abruptly as from 31 January 1933 when a rail strike provided the excuse to do so. The last goods services ceased on 3 July 1950, the LMS having been nationalised along with the majority of other British railways in 1948 and the NCC sold back to the Northern Ireland government to become part of the UTA.

MAP 20

1 JANUARY 1920

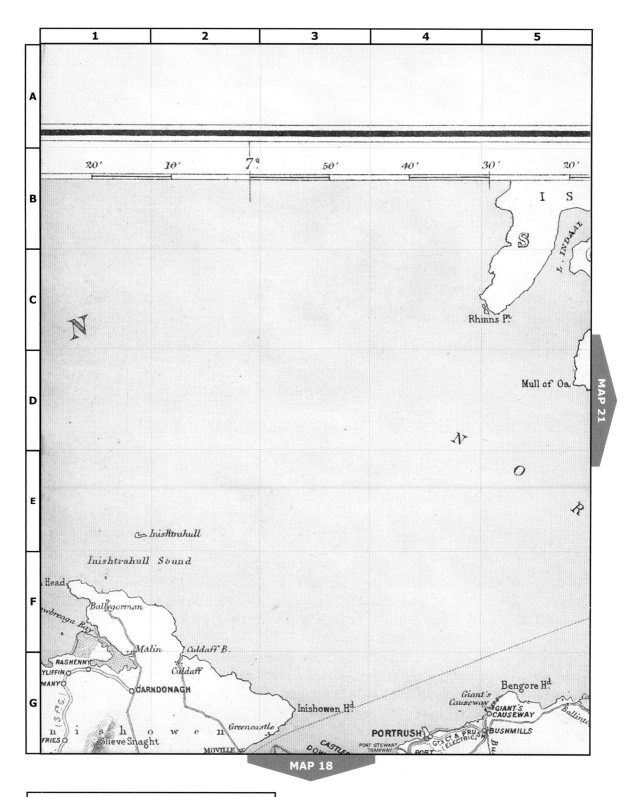

	1	2	3	4	5

20'   10'   7º   50'   40'   30'   20'

N

Rhinns Pt.

Mull of Oa.

N

O

R

Inishtrahull

Inishtrahull Sound

Head

Ballygorman

Malin   *Culdaff B.*

RASHENNY

YLIFFIN   *Culdaff*

MANY

CARNDONAGH

Bengore Hd.

Giant's
Causeway   GIANT'S
CAUSEWAY

Ballinto

BUSHMILLS

Inishowen Hd.

FRIES   i n i s h o w e n   *Greencastle*

Slieve Snaght

PORTRUSH

PORT STEWART
TRAMWAY   Gʸ Cᵗ & PRUˢ
ELECTRIC Sᴴ

PORT

MOVILLE

CASTLE
DOW

MAP 21

MAP 18

LEGEND

All lines 3ft gauge except:
5ft 3in gauge BELFAST & NORTHERN COUNTIES RAILWAY (G4)

G4 PORT STEWART TRAMWAY should be: PORTSTEWART TRAMWAY
G4 PORT STEWART should be PORTSTEWART

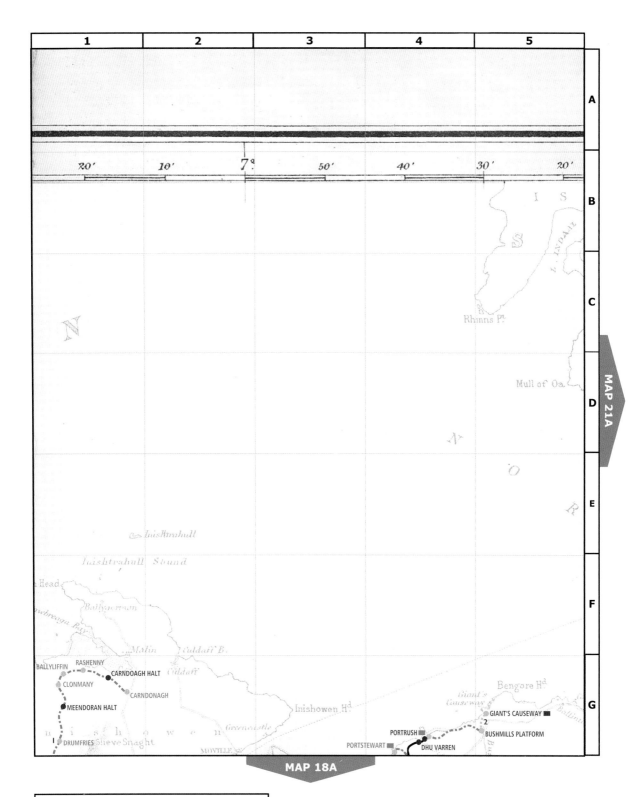

MAP 21A

MAP 18A

LEGEND

1 DRUMFRIES: Station building now part of the North Pole Bar
2 3ft gauge GIANT'S CAUSEWAY & BUSHMILLS RAILWAY.
www.freewebs.com/giantscausewayrailway/

GIANT'S CAUSEWAY AND PORTRUSH ELECTRIC TRAMWAY

WORLD'S FIRST HYDRO ELECTRIC TRAMWAY — OPENED IN 1883

TIME TABLE from 6th JULY, 1949
UNTIL FURTHER NOTICE

Tramcars between Portrush, Bushmills and Giant's Causeway will run as follows:—

WEEK DAYS			SUNDAYS		
Portrush to Bushmills and Giant's Causeway	Giant's Causeway to Bushmills and Portrush	Bushmills to Portrush	Portrush to Bushmills and Giant's Causeway	Giant's Causeway to Bushmills and Portrush	Bushmills to Portrush
10.30 a.m.	——	8.15 a.m.	10.30 a.m.	——	9.45 a.m.
11.20 ,,	——	9.45 ,,	12. 0 noon	——	10.45 ,,
12.45 p.m.	——	10.30 ,,	1.10 p.m.	——	11.45 ,,
1.30 ,,	11.20 a.m.	11.30 ,,	2.10 ,,	12.15 p.m.	12.25 p.m.
2.10 ,,	12.20 p.m.	12.30 p.m.	2.40 ,,	1. 0 ,,	1.10 ,,
2.40 ,,	1.35 ,,	1.45 ,,	3.10 ,,	2. 0 ,,	2.10 ,,
3.10 ,,	2.20 ,,	2.30 ,,	3.50 ,,	3. 0 ,,	3.10 ,,
3.40 ,,	3. 0 ,,	3.10 ,,	4.30 ,,	4. 0 ,,	4.10 ,,
4.10 ,,	4. 0 ,,	4.10 ,,	5.15 ,,	4.45 ,,	4.55 ,,
5.15 ,,	4.45 ,,	4.55 ,,	6. 0 ,,	5. 0 ,,	5.10 ,,
6. 0 ,,	5. 0 ,,	5.10 ,,	6.30 ,,	5.30 ,,	5.40 ,,
6.40 ,,	6.10 ,,	6.20 ,,	7.15 ,,	6.10 ,,	6.20 ,,
7.10 ,,	7. 0 ,,	7.10 ,,	X8.15 ,,	7.20 ,,	7.30 ,,
8. 0 ,,	8. 0 ,,	8.10 ,,			
X9. 0 ,,					

X—Bushmills only   X—Bushmills only

SPECIAL EXCURSION TICKETS

Will be issued from Bushmills to Portrush Daily by all Tramcars at fare of 1/2 Return, available for day of issue only.

SUBSCRIPTION MONTHLY AND WEEKLY TICKETS

Are issued at Reduced Rates, also Special Rates for School Children and Special Parties, on application to Tramway Office, Portrush. Special Tramcars can be engaged on application.

Travel by Electric Tramcars, the best means of viewing the beautiful coast and enjoying the magnificent scenery.

NOTE.—This Time Table is liable to alteration, if found necessary without notice from the Company.

The Company will not hold themselves responsible for Tramcars not starting at the times appointed, nor for delays that may occur on the road.

The Cars have special stopping places, indicated by sign, "CARS STOP HERE." Passengers are requested to meet the Cars at those places and are cautioned not to get on or off the Cars while in motion.

FARES

			Single Fare	*Return Fare
Portrush and Giant's Causeway			1s 9d	3s 0d
,, ,,	Bushmills	...	1s 0d	1s 6d
,, ,,	Dunluce Castle	...	9d	1s 0d
,, ,,	Portballintrae	...	10d	1s 3d
Bushmills and Dunluce Castle		...	9d	1s 0d
,, ,,	Giant's Causeway		6d	
Portrush and White Rocks		...	6d	
,, ,,	Golf Club	...	3d	

* Return Tickets are available for One Month from day of issue.

G. F. MEARA, Engineer/Manager.

Portrush, 6th July, 1949.   Telephone: Portrush 2318.

ITINERARY

The Tramway runs along the verge of the cliffs, skirting the blue waters of the North Atlantic for almost the entire distance to the Causeway.

Leaving Portrush the line rises by a gentle gradient to the White Rocks, where a magnificent view is obtained.

To the westward rise Innishowen and Malin Head, while the Skerries lie in the foreground, with the Island of Islay, off the Scottish coast, on the horizon.

The coast line is a succession of beautiful caves worn out by the waves of the Atlantic. Further along, at the Punch Bowl, where a sharp curve in the Tramway Track occurs, one can look down into the so-called Cathedral Cave.

A little further eastward is the Giant's Head, a gigantic profile in the white limestone rock, with a small crown of black basalt on its head.

The next siding affords a glimpse of a charming bay with the "Lion's Paw," a narrow ridge, running seaward, and the Wishing Arch, a perfect white limestone arch, spanning the deep blue water.

The summit, at 193 feet above sea level, is reached at Clooney Hill.

The next point of interest is Dunluce Castle, standing isolated on a projecting spur of basalt. This ancient stronghold of the MacQuillans has lately been taken over by the Northern Government, scheduled as an "ancient monument" and partially restored.

A mile farther along, below the Tramway line and close to the sea, lies Portballintrae, a small but favourite watering-place with excellent bathing and angling.

Bushmills is next passed, famous for its whiskey. Here, about three-quarters of a mile from the town, on the banks of the River Bush, amid charming surroundings, is situated the Hydro Electric Generating Station which supplies the Electricity to the Tramway.

Visitors to the district are cordially invited to visit this station, the first in the world to use "the waste waters of a river" to generate electricity for traction purposes and thereby gaining for the Tramway the distinction of being the Pioneer Hydro Electric Tramway of the World.

A pleasant run through the sand-hills now brings the traveller to the Giant's Causeway.

"There is nothing in the world like the Giant's Causeway," where "the rocks are cut as by a mathematical calculation." Most of the pillars are six-sided, some have five sides, a few four sides, fewer still have three and seven sides, and only one, the "Key Stone," has eight sides.

In the "Wishing Chair," the "Giant's Organ," the "Giant's Loom" and the "Honeycomb," to mention only a few examples, the sections of the pillars can best be seen. The "Giant's Well" always gives a constant flow of deliciously cool and sparkling water.

Famous also are the Causeway caves, one of them measuring 700 feet long with a height of 60 feet.

From the 6 July 1949 GCPBVT timetable leaflet, giving details of services, fares and tickets – plus a fulsome description of the tramway's route and neighbouring points of interest for tourists. Sadly, such publicity could not prevent the line's closure later that year.

THE GIANT'S CAUSEWAY, PORTRUSH & BUSH VALLEY TRAMWAY

The Giant's Causeway Tramway – to give it its common name – was authorised by the Giant's Causeway, Portrush and Bush Valley Railway and Tramways Act 1880 and opened on 29 January 1883 as a 3ft gauge street and roadside steam tramway; steam haulage was a stop-gap measure until regular electric operation began on 5 November 1883 with current supplied by an outside conductor rail – one of the first such traction systems in the British Isles. (This somewhat dangerous method of current supply was replaced on 26 July 1899 by an overhead wire.)

The first section opened ran from the street outside the BNCR station at Portrush along or beside the road to Bushmills, 6 miles to the east; an extension opened on 1 July 1887 took the tramway through the fields to a terminus by the famous Giant's Causeway, nearly 3 miles to the north. Closure, in the face of increasing road competition, came on 30 September 1949 – though more than half a century later Easter 2002 saw the reopening of the Bushmills – Giant's Causeway section as a 3ft gauge tourist railway. The works and main depot were at Portrush, with a smaller depot at Bushmills.

An anonymous postcard of Portrush's impressive standard gauge station, with the sea immediately beyond. In the foreground a 3ft gauge GCPBVR train of two trailers headed by powered toast rack No.21 (company-built of 1899) is about to set off on its journey along the coast.   *K. Turner Collection*

THE PORTSTEWART TRAMWAY

The Portstewart Tramway was a 3ft gauge single-track street and roadside steam tramway built under an 1880 Order-in-Council to link the seaside resort of Portstewart with the BNCR mainline station of that name a little under 2 miles inland. The termini were simply dead-end tracks outside the railway station at one end and outside the Montague Hotel on The Parade at the other (by the depot). The line was opened officially on 28 June 1882 and was closed on 30 January 1926, by which time it had been absorbed in turn by the BNCR (1897), the MR (1903) and finally the LMS (1923).

MAP 21

1 JANUARY 1920

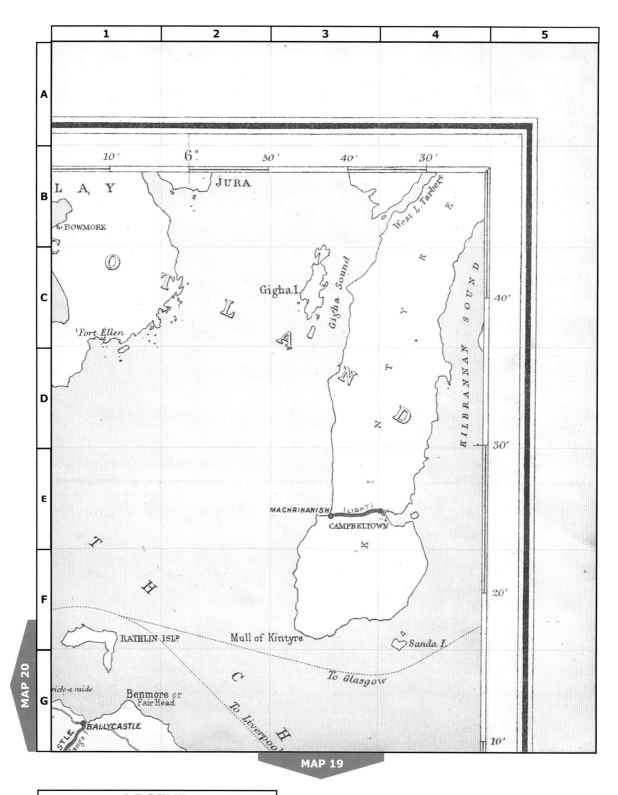

LEGEND

BALLYCASTLE RAILWAY (G1) 3ft gauge
CAMPBELTOWN & MACHRIHANISH RAILWAY (E3 – E4) 2ft 3in gauge

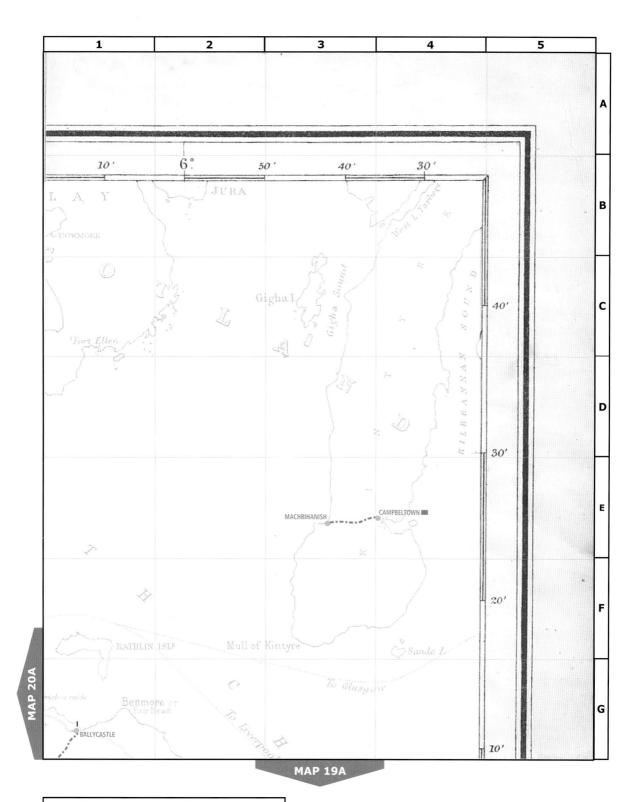

MAP 20A

MAP 19A

LEGEND

1 BALLYCASTLE: Part of site cleared as a car park at the start of the MOYLE WAY. www.walkni.com

Ballycastle station, right, the northern terminus of the BR, on a Lawrence of Dublin tinted postcard. Centre is the stone bridge over the River Tow – a bridge that had to be repaired even before the railway opened after being found to be cracked.   *K.Turner Collection*

THE BALLYCASTLE RAILWAY

The Ballycastle Railway Company, incorporated by Act of Parliament on 22 July 1878, operated a 3ft gauge single line railway running north-east from its own platform in the BNCR station at Ballymoney to the coastal town of its title, just over 16 miles away. The railway opened in 1880 (probably on 18 October) and ran until financial pressures brought about its closure from 24 March 1924; the NCC thereupon took over its working, reopening the line on 11 August that year. It consequently passed into the control of the UTA, in 1948, and was closed two years later as from 3 July 1950 (with the final trains running the day before).

BALLYCASTLE RAILWAY.

For the information of the Public the Trains on Ballycastle Railway are given underneath, but the Northern Counties Committee of the Midland Railway do not accept any responsibility for the observance of the Time Table.

STATIONS.		WEEK DAYS										SUNDAYS	
		a m	a m		p m		p m					p.m.	
BALLYCASTLE	dep	7 0	11 0	Thurs. only.	2 15	Runs Ballycastle Fair Days.	3 15	..	••	••	••	4 55	••
Capecastle	,,	7 11	11 11		2 26		3 25	..	••	••	••	5 5	••
Armoy ..	,,	7 22	11 22		2 37		3 33	..	••	••	••	5 13	••
Stranocum	,,	7 34	11 34		2 49		3 43	..	••	••	••	5 23	••
Dervock ..	,,	7 43	11 43		2 58		3 50	•	••	••	••	5 30	••
BALLYMONEY ..	arr	8 0	12 0		3 15		4 5	..	••	••	••	5 45	••

DOWN TRAINS TO BALLYCASTLE.

STATIONS.		WEEK DAYS										SUNDAYS	
		am	a.m.		p.m.		p m					a m	
BALLYMONEY ..	dep	9 0	10 40	Runs Ballycastle Fair Days.	1 30	Thurs. only.	7 0	••	••	••		10 45	••
Dervock ..	,,	9 17	10 57		1 47		7 14	••	••	••		10 59	••
Stranocum	,,	9 26	11 6		1 56		7 21	••	••	••		11 6	••
Armoy ..	,,	9 38	11 18		2 8		7 32	••	••	••		11 17	••
Capecastle	,,	9 49	11 29		2 19		7 41	••	••	••		11 26	••
BALLYCASTLE	arr	10 0	11 40		2 30		7 50	••	••	••		11 35	••

A BR public timetable of 1918. Note the punctuality disclaimer of its bigger neighbour!

THE CAMPBELTOWN & MACHRIHANISH LIGHT RAILWAY

And finally... although not in Ireland, the 2ft 3in gauge Campbeltown & Machrihanish Light Railway appears on the RCH map by virtue of its geographical proximity to County Antrim. Indeed, its isolated position on the Mull of Kintyre meant that during its lifetime (August 1906 – May 1932) it was always closer to the Irish railway network than to the Scottish. Despite this proximity however, the port of Campbeltown never boasted a passenger steamer service across the narrow North Channel to Ireland, only up the Firth of Clyde to Glasgow.

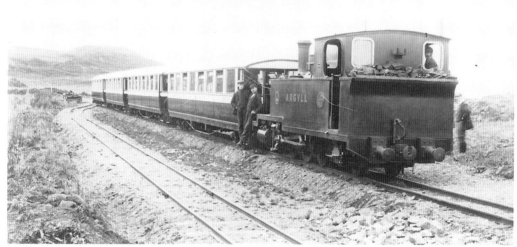

The Campbeltown & Machrihanish Light Railway - a railway not so far removed, in many senses, from its Irish narrow gauge neighbours. Here *Argyll* (Andrew Barclay 1049 of 1906) and train wait to depart from the sand dunes of Machrihanish as captured on a Locomotive Publishing Co Ltd postcard.   *K. Turner Collection*

Campbeltown was well served by sea from Glasgow, as this advertisement from a 1922 *Bradshaw's* (or, to give it its full title, *Bradshaw's General Railway and Steam Navigation Guide for Great Britain and Ireland*) shows, but not from Ireland.

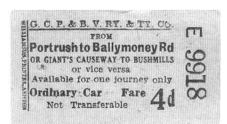

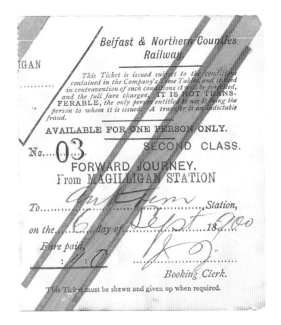
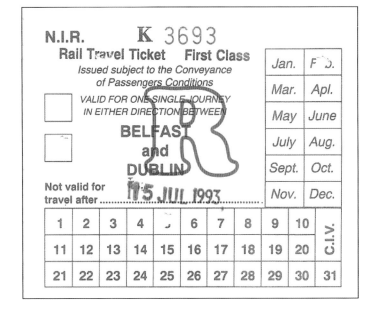

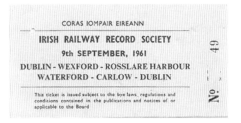

Another selection of Irish railway tickets, this time including some of the more utilitarian styles adopted in the latter years of the 20th Century.

GAZETTEER I – 1920 Stations

Map references of stations open as of 1 January 1920, indexed alphabetically letter by letter, together with their name at time of opening (if different). Adjacent stations sharing a common name are normally accorded the one entry.

A

ABBEYDORNEY 3 D5
ABBEYFEALE 4 D2
ABBEYLEIX 11 F1
ABOHILL 14A A4
ACHILL 13 Inset A1

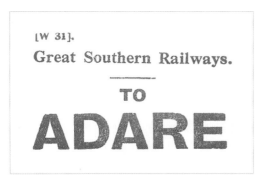

ADARE 4 B4
ADAVOYLE 15 C5
ADELAIDE & WINDSOR 19 F2
ADOON 14 D4
AGHADOWEY 18 B4
ALDERGROVE 19 E1
ANNADALE 14 C3
ANNAGHMORE 18 G4
ANTRIM [GNR(I)] 19 D1
ANTRIM [NCC] 19 D1
  Also known as ANTRIM JUNCTION
ARDAGH 4 C3
ARDARA ROAD HALT 17 E1
  Originally named ARDARA ROAD
ARDEE 15 E5
ARDFERT 3 D5
ARDGLASS 16 A4
ARDMAYLE 5 B4
ARDMORE 18 B3
ARDRAHAN 9 D4
ARDSOLLUS & QUIN 9 G4

ARIGNA 14 C3
ARKLOW 12 G2
ARMAGH RAILWAY STREET 15 A4
  Also known as ARMAGH

ARMOY 18 A5
ARVA ROAD 15 D1
ASHTOWN 12 B1
ASKEATON 4 B3
ATHBOY 15 G3
ATHENRY 9 C5
ATHLONE 10 B3
ATHY 11 E3
ATTANAGH 11 G1
ATTYMON JUNCTION 9 C5
  Originally named ATTYMON
AUGHACASLA 3 E4
AUGHAVILLE 1A C2
AUGHER 18 G2
AUGHNACLOY 18 G3
AUGHRIM 12 G1
AUNASCAUL 3 E3
AVOCA 12 G1
  Originally named OVOCA

B

BAGENALSTOWN 6 A3
  Originally named BAGNALSTOWN
BALBRIGGAN 16 G1
BALLA 13 E3
BALLAGHADEREEN 13 E5
BALLARENA 18 A3
BALLINA 13 C3
BALLINAHOUN 10A B4
  Originally named DOON,
  also known as BALLINAHOWN. Race traffic only
BALLINAMALLARD 17 G5
BALLINAMORE (County Donegal) 17 C3
BALLINAMORE (County Leitrim) 14 C4
BALLINASCARTHY [CBSCR] 1 C4
  Originally named BALLINASCARTY
BALLINASCARTHY [TCR] 1 C4
BALLINASLOE 10 B2
BALLINASTEENIG 3 F3
BALLINCOLIG 1 A5
BALLINDANGAN 5 E2
BALLINDERRY 19 F1
BALLINDINE 13 G4
BALLINDRAIT 17 C5
BALLINEED & ENNISKEAN 1 B4
BALLINGLEN 12 G1
BALLINGRANE 4 B4
  Originally named RATHKEALE
BALLINHASSIG 1 B5
BALLINLOUGH 13 F5
BALLINMORE HALT
BALLINOSARE 3 F3

BALLINROBE 13 G3
BALLINTOGHER 14 B1
BALLINTRA 17 F2
BALLYARDS 15 A4
BALLYBAY 15 C3
BALLYBEG 15 F4
Also known as BALLYBEG CROSSING
BALLYBOFFEY 17 D4
BALLYBOLEY 19 D2
Originally BALLYCLARE JUNCTION;
also known as BALLYBOLEY JUNCTION
BALLYBRACK 4 F1
BALLYBROPHY 10 F5
Originally named BORRIS & ROSCREA JUNCTION
BALLYBUNION 3 B5
BALLYCAR 9 G4
Originally named BALLYCAR & NEWMARKET
BALLYCARRY 19 D3
BALLYCASTLE 21 G1
BALLYCLARE 19 D2
BALLYCLARE JUNCTION 19 E2
Originally named BALLYNURE ROAD
BALLYCLOUGHAN 19 C1
BALLYCONNELL 14 C5
BALLYCULLANE 6 E4
BALLYCUMBER 10 B5
Originally named PROSPECT
BALLYDEHOB 1 D1
BALLYDOUGHERTY HALT 15 A5
BALLYDUFF (County Leitrim) 14 C4
BALLYDUFF (County Waterford) 5 F3
BALLYEASTON HALT 19 D2
Originally named BALLEASTON BRIDGE
BALLYGARVEY 19 C1
BALLYGAWLEY (County Sligo) 14A B1
Also known as BALLYGAWLEY MARKET PLATFORM
BALLYGAWLEY (County Tyrone) 18 G2
BALLYGLUNIN 9 B4
BALLYGOWAN 19 F3
BALLYHAISE 15 C1
Originally named BELTURBET JUNCTION
BALLYHALE 6 C2
BALLYHAUNIS 13 F5
BALLYHEADY 14 C5
BALLYHOOLY 5 F1
BALLYKELLY 18 B2
BALLYKINLAR HALT 16A Inset F3
Military traffic only
BALLYLIFFIN 20 G1
BALLYMACARRETT HALT 19A Inset B4
BALLYMAGAN 18 A1
BALLYMAGORRY 18 C1
BALLYMARTLE 1 B5
BALLYMENA 19 C1
BALLYMOE 14 F1
BALLYMONEY 18 A5

BALLYMOTE 14 C1
BALLYMURRY 14 G3
BALLYNAHINCH (County Down) 19 G3
BALLYNAHINCH (County Galway) 8 A5
BALLYNAHINCH JUNCTION 19 G3
BALLYNASHEE 19 D2
BALLYNOE 16 A3
BALLYNURE 19 D2
BALLYRAGGET 11 G1
BALLYROBERT HALT 19 D2
Originally named BALLYPALADY
BALLYRONEY 16 A2
BALLYSHANNON 17 F2
BALLYSODARE 14 B1
BALLYVARY 13 E3
BALLYWARD 16 A2
BALLYWILLAN 15 E1
BALLY WILLIAM 6 C3
Originally named BALLYWILLIAM FOR NEW ROSS
BALMORAL 19 F2
BALTIMORE 1 D1
BALTINGLASS 11 F4
BANAGHER 10 D3
BANBRIDGE 16 A1
BANDON 1 B5
BANGOR 19 E3
BANSHA 5 C3
BANTEER 4 F4
BANTRY 1 C1
BARNAGH 4 C3
BARNESMORE HALT 17 E3
Originally named BARRACK BRIDGE HALT
BASIN 3 E5
BATTERSTOWN 11 A5
BAWNBY ROAD & TEMPLEPORT 14 C5
BEAUPARK 15 F5
BECTIVE 15 G4
BEKAN 13 F4
BELCOO 14 A4
Also known as BELCOO & BLACKLION

BELFAST GREAT VICTORIA STREET 19 E2
Originally named BELFAST
BELFAST QUEEN'S QUAY 19 E2
Also known as QUEEN'S QUAY
BELLARENA 18 A3

BELLEEK 17 G3
BELLURGAN 16 C1
BELMONT & CLOGHAN 10 C4
BELTURBET 15 C1
BENNETTSBRIDGE 6 B2
   Originally named BENNETSBRIDGE
BERAGH 18 F2
BESSBROOK [BNT] 15 B5
BESSBROOK [GNR(I)] 15 B5
   Originally named NEWRY
BIRDHILL 10 G1
BIRR 10 E4
   Originally named PARSONSTOWN
BISHOPSTOWN 2 A1
BLACKROCK (County Cork) 2 A1
BLACKROCK (County Dublin) 12 C2
BLACKWEIR 4 A1
BLANCHARDSTOWN 12 B1
BLARNEY [CMLR] 1 A5
BLARNEY (GSWR] 4 G5
BLENNERVILLE 3 E5
BLESSINGTON 11 D5
BLOOMFIELD 19 E3
BONER 5 B1
BOOTERSTOWN 12 C1
BORRIS 6 B3
BOYLE 14 D2
BRAY 12 D2
BRIDGE END 18 B1

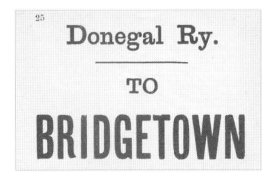

BRIDGETOWN 6 E5
BRIDGETOWN HALT 17 E3
BRITTAS 11 C5
BROIGHTER 18 A3
BROOKEBOROUGH 15 A1
BROOKMOUNT 19 F1
BROSNA 10 E4
   Also known as BROSNA HALT
BRUCKLESS 17 E1
BRUREE 4 C5
BUNCRANA 17 A5
BUNDORAN 17 G2
BUNDORAN JUNCTION 17 G5
   Originally named LOWTHERSTOWN ROAD
BURNFOOT 18 B1
BURNT MILL 4 G5

BURTONPORT 17 B1
BUSH 16 D1
BUSHMILLS 20 G5
BUTTEVANT & DONERAILE 4 E5

C

CAHIR 5 D4
CAHIRCIVEEN 3 G3
   Also timetabled as CAHIRCIVEEN FOR WATERVILLE
CALEDON 15 A3
CAMOLIN 7 B1
CAMP 3 E4
CAMPBELTOWN (Scotland) 21 E4
CAMPILE 6 E3
CAPECASTLE 19 A1
CAPPA 4 A1
CAPPAGH 5 F4
CAPPOQUIN 5 F4
CARRAGH LAKE FOR GLENCAR 3 F4
CARBURY 11 B3
   Originally named CARBERRY
CARGAN 19 B1
CARLINGFORD 16 C1
CARLOW 11 G3
CARNAGH 15 B4
CARNALEA 19 E3
CARNDONAGH 20 G1
CARRICHUE 18 B2
   Originally named CARRICKHUGH
CARRICKFERGUS 19 D3
CARRICKMACROSS 15 D4
CARRICKMINES 12 C2
CARRICKMORE 18 F2
CARRICK-ON-SHANNON 14 D3
CARRICK-ON-SUIR 6 D1
CARRIGALINE 2 B1
CARRIGALOE 2 A2
CARRIGANS 18 C1
CARRIGROHANE 1 A5
CARRIGTWOHILL 2 A2
   Originally named CARRIGTOHILL
CARROLL'S CROSS 6 E1
CARROWEN 17 B5
CARROWMORE 13 C5
CASHEL 5 B4
CASHELNAGORE 17 A3
CASTLEBAR 13 E2
CASTLEBELLINGHAM 15 D5
CASTLEBLAYNEY 15 C4
   Originally named CASTLEBLANEY
CASTLECALDWELL 17 F3
CASTLECONNELL 5 A1
CASTLEDERG 17 D5
CASTLEDAWSON 18 D4
CASTLEFINN 17 D5
   Also known as CASTLEFIN

CASTLEGREGORY 3 E4
CASTLEGREGORY JUNCTION 3 E4
CASTLEGRAVE 13 G4
CASTLEISLAND 4 E1
CASTLEMAINE 3 E5
CASTLEREA 14 F1
CASTLEROCK 18 A3
CASTLETOWN 10 A5
CASTLETOWNROCHE 5 F1
CASTLEWELLAN 16 A2
CAVAN 15 D1
CHAPEL 6 C4
  Also timetabled as CHAPEL FOR CLONROCHE
CHARLESTOWN 13 D5
CHARLEVILLE 4 D5
  Named RATHLUIRC 1920s – 1990
CHURCH CROSS 1 D2
CHURCHILL 17 B4
CLADY 17 D5
CLARA 10 B5
CLAR BRIDGE HALT 17 E3
CLARE CASTLE 9 G4
CLAREMORRIS 13 F4
CLIFDEN 8 A4
CLOGHAN 17 C3
CLOGHER 18 G2
CLOGHROE 1 A5
CLONAKILTY 1 C4
CLONAKILTY JUNCTION 1 B4
CLONDAKIN 12 B1
CLONDULANE 5 F2
  Originally named GLENWICK
CLONES 15 B2
CLONHUGH 15 G1
CLONMANY 20 G1
CLONMEL 5 D5
CLONSILLA 11 B5
CLONTARF 12 B1
CLOUGHJORDAN 10 F3
CLOUGH ROAD 19 B1
COACHFORD 1 A4
COACHFORD JUNCTION 1 A5
  Originally named BLARNEY JUNCTION
COALISLAND 18 F4
COLBINSTOWN 11 E4
COLEBROOKE 15 A1
COLERAINE 18 A4
  Originally named COLERAINE (NORTHBROOK)
COLLIN HALT 19 D2
COLLOONEY [GSWR] 14 B1
COLLOONEY [MGWR] 14 B1
COLLOONEY [SLNCR] 14 B1
COMBER 19 F3
CONVOY 17 C5
COOKSTOWN 18 E4

COOKSTOWN JUNCTION 19 D1
  Originally named DRUMSOUGH
COOLAGHY HALT 17 C5
COOTEHILL 15 C2
CORBET 16 A1

L. M. & S. R.
Cork

CORK ALBERT QUAY 2 A1
CORK ALBERT STREET 2 A1
CORK CAPWELL 2 A1
CORK GLANMIRE ROAD 2 A1
CORK WESTERN ROAD 2 A1
CORNABRONE 14 C4
CORNAGILLAGH HALT 17 C5
COROFIN 9 F3
COURTMACSHERRY 1 C5
CRAGGAKNOCK 9 G1
CRAIGAVAD 19 E3
CRATLOE 4 A4
CRAUGHWELL & LOUGHREA 9 C5
CREAGH (County Cork) 1 D2
CREAGH (County Leitrim) 14 C3
CREAGHANROE 15 B4
CREESLOUGH 17 A4
CREEVY HALT 17 F2
CREW 17 D5
CROLLY 17 B2
CROOKSTOWN ROAD 1 A4
  Originally named CROOKSTOWN & RYECOURT
CROOM 4 B5
CROSSDONKEY 15 D1
CROSSGAR 19 G3
CROSSHAVEN 2 B2
CROSS ROADS 19 B1
CRUMLIN 19 E1
CRUSHEEN 9 F4
CULLION 18 C1
CULLOVILLE 15 C4
CULLYBACKEY 18 C5
CULMORE 18 B1
CULTRA 19 E3
CURRAGH BRIDGE HALT 18A B4
CURRAGH MAINLINE 11A D3
CURRAGH SIDING 11A D3
  Also known as CURRAGH RACECOURSE PLATFORM;
  for race and military traffic only
CURRAHEEN 3 E5
CURRY 13 D5

D

DALKEY 12 C2
DEELIS 3 E4
DERG BRIDGE HALT 17 D3
DEREEN 14 E4
DERRIAGHY HALT 19 F2
DERRYMORE 3 E4
DERRYORK 18 B3
DERVOCK 18 A5
DESERT 1 B4
DESERTMARTIN 18 D4
DESERTONE HALT 18 C1
DEVON ROAD 4 D2
DINGLE 3 F2
DOAGH [ng] 19 D2
DOAGH [std g] 19 D2
  Originally named BALLYPALLADY
DONABATE 12 A2
DONAGHADEE 19 E4
DONAGHMORE 18 F3
DONAMON 14 G2
DONEGAL 17 E3
DONEMANA 18 C1
DONOUGHMORE 4 G5
DOOKS 3 F4
DOONBEG 4 A1
DOONISKEY 1 A4
DOORIN ROAD 17 E2
DOWNHILL 18 A3
DOWNPATRICK 16 A3
DOWNPATRICK LOOP PLATFORM 16A Inset F4
DRAPERSTOWN 18 D4
DRIMOLEAUGE 1 C2
DRINEY 14A C3
  Also known as DRINEY CURVE. *For excursion trains only*
DRIPSEY 1 A5
DROGHEDA 16 F1
DROMAHAIR 14 B2
DROMKEEN 5 B1
DROMIN JUNCTION 15 E5
DROMOD 14 E4
DROMORE 19 G1
DROMORE ROAD 18 G1
DRUMBAR HALT 17 E3
DRUMFRIES 20 G1
DRUMHOWNA 15 E1
  Also timetabled as DRUMHOWNAGH
DRUMREE 11 A5
DRUMSHANBO 14 C3
DRUMSNA 14 D3
DRUMSURN 18 B3
DUBLIN AMIENS STREET 12 B1
DUBLIN BROADSTONE 12 B1
DUBLIN HARCOURT STREET 12 B1

DUBLIN KINGSBRIDGE 12 B1
DUBLIN NORTH WALL 12 B1
DUBLIN WESTLAND ROW 12 B1
DULEEK 15 G5
DUNADRY 19 E1
DUNBOYNE 11 B5
DUNCORMICK 6 E4

C. & L. R.
DUNDALK

DUNDALK JUNCTION 15 D5
  Originally named DUNDALK
DUNDALK QUAY STREET 15 D5
DUNDONALD 19 E3
DUNDRUM (County Down) 16 A3
DUNDRUM (County Dublin) 12 C1
DUNDRUM (County Tipperary) 5 B3
DUNFANAGHY ROAD 17 A3
DUNGANNON 18 F4
DUNGARVAN 5 F5
DUNGIVEN 18 C3
DUNGLOE 17 B1
  Originally named LOUGHMEALA
DUNKETTLE 2 A1
DUNKINEELY 17 E1
DUNLAVIN 11 E4
DUNLEER 15 E5
DUNLOY 18 B5
DUNMANWAY 1 B3
DUNMURRY 19 F2
DUNSANDLE 9 C5
DURROW 6 F1
  Also known as DURROW & STRADBALLY
DURRUS ROAD 1 C1

E

EDENDERRY 11 B3
EDERMINE FERRY 6 C5
EDGEWORTHTON 14 F5
  Also known as MOSTRIM
EDMONDSTOWN 14 D1
EGLINTON 18 B2
EMALOUGH 3 E4
EMBANKMENT 11 C5
EMLY 5 C2
ENFIELD 11 B4
ENNIS [GSWR] 9 G4
ENNIS [WCR] 9 G4
ENNISCORTHY 6 C5
ENNISKILLEN 14 A5
ENNISTYMON 9 F2
ESSEXFORD 15 D4

F

FAHAN 17 A5
FAIRYHOUSE BRIDGE 11A A5
FALCARRAGH 17 A3
FARRANALEEN 5 C4
FARRANFORE 4 E1
FARRANGALWAY 2 B1
FENAGH 14 D4
FENIT 3 D4
FERBANE 10 C4
FERMOY 5 F2
FERNS 6 B5
FERNS LOCK 11 B4
FETHARD 5 C5
FIDDOWN 6 D1
  Also known as FIDDOWN & PORTLAW
FINAGHY HALT 19 F2
FINTONA 18 G1
FINTONA JUNCTION 18 F1
FINTOWN 17 C3
FIRMOUNT 4 G5
FIVEMILETOWN 18 G1
FLOAT 15 F1
  Also timetabled as FLOAT, CASTLEPOLLARD

S. L. & N. C. Railway Company

TO

FLORENCECOURT

FLORENCECOURT 14 A4
FOTA 2 A2
  Originally named FOATY
FOXFORD 13 D3
FOXHALL 17 B4
FOXROCK 12 C2
  Originally named LEOPARDSTOWN;
  also timetabled as FOXROCK FOR LEOPARDSTOWN
FOX'S BRIDGE 4 G5

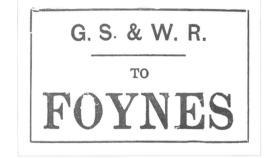

G. S. & W. R.

TO

FOYNES

FOYNES 4 B3
FRANCIS ROAD 3A B5

FYFIN 17 D5

G

GALLAGH ROAD 18 B1
GALWAY 9 C3
GARADICE 14 C4
GARNDONAGH 20 G1
GARRYNADOUR 3 F3
GARVAGH 18 B4
GEASHILL 11 D1
GIANT'S CAUSEWAY 20 G5
GIBBSTOWN 15 F4
GLANWORTH 5 E1
GLARRYFORD 18 B5
GLASLOUGH 15 A3
  Also timetabled as GLASSLOUGH
GLASNEVIN JUNCTION 12 B1
GLENAGEARY 12 C2
GLENAVY 19 F1
GLENBEIGH 3 F4
GLENBROOK 2 A2
GLENEALY 12 F2

S. L. & N. C. Railway Company

To

Glenfarne

GLENFARNE 14 A3
GLENMAQUIN 17 C5
GLENMORE (County Donegal) 17 D4
GLENMORE (County Kerry) 3 E4
GLENMORE & AYLWARDSTOWN 6 D3
  Originally named AYLWARDSTOWN
GLENTIES 17 D2
GLOUNAGALT BRIDGE 3 E4
GLYNN 19 C3
GOLF HALT or PLATFORM 17A A5
GOOLD'S CROSS 5 B3
GORAGHWOOD 15 B5
  Originally named GORAGH WOOD
GORESBRIDGE 6 A3
GOREY 7 A1
GORMANSTON 16 G1
GORT 9 E4
GORTATLEA 4 E1
GOWRAN 6 A2
GRACEHILL 18 A5
GRANGE 6 D2
GRANGE CON 11 E4

MAGILLIGAN 18 A3
MAGUIRESBRIDGE [CVT] 15 A1
MAGUIRESBRIDGE [GNR(I)] 14 A5
  Originally named MAGUIRE'S BRIDGE
MALAHIDE 12 A2
MALLARANNY 13 Inset A1
MALLOW 4 F5
MANORCUNNINGHAM 17 B5
  Also timetabled as MANOR
MANORHAMPTON 14 A2
MANULLA JUNCTION 13 E3
MARINO 19 E3
MARKETHILL 15 A5
MARYBOROUGH 11 E1
MAYNOOTH 11 B5
MAZE 19 F2
  Originally named MAZE PLATFORM
MEENGLAS HALT 17 D4
  Closed c.1918 – c.1936
MIDLETON 2 A3
  Originally named MIDLETON, BALLINACURRA & CLOYNE
MILFORD (County Armagh) 15 A4
MILFORD (County Carlow) 11 G3
MILLSTREET 4 F3
MILLTOWN (County Dublin) 12 C1
MILLTOWN (County Galway) 13 G4
  Also timetabled as MILLTOWN (GALWAY)
MILLTOWN (County Kerry) 3 F5
MILTOWN MALBAY 9 G2
  Also known as MILTOWN-MALBAY

MITCHELSTOWN 5 E2
MOATE 10 B4
MOGEELY 2 A3
MOHILL 14 D4
MOIRA 19 F1
MOLAHIFFE 4 E1
MONAGHAN 15 A3
MONAGHAN ROAD 15 B3
MONASTEREVAN 11 D3
MONEYCARRIE HALT 18 B4
MONEYMORE 18 E4
MONKSTOWN 2 A1
MONKSTOWN HALT 19 E2
MOORFIELDS 19 C1
MORLEY'S BRIDGE 1 A2
MOSSLEY 19 E2

MOUNTAIN STAGE 3 G4
MOUNTCHARLES 17 E2
MOUNTMELLICK 11 D1
MOUNT PLEASANT 15 C5
  Originally named PLASTER
MOUNTRATH & CASTLETOWN 11 F1
MOURNE ABBEY 4 F5
MOYASTA JUNCTION 4 A1
MOYCULLEN 9 B3
MOYVALLEY 11 B3
MUCKMORE HALT 19 E1
MULLAFERNAGHAN 19 G1
MULLANBOY HALT 17A E2
MULLINAVAT 6 D2
MULLINGAR 11 A1
MULTYFARNHAM 15 G1

N

NAAS 11 C4
NARROW WATER 16 C1
NAVAN 15 G4
NAVAN JUNCTION 15 G4
NEILL'S HILL 19 E3
NENAGH 10 G2
NEWBLISS 15 B2
NEWBRIDGE 11 D4
NEWBROOK RACECOURSE 11A A1
NEW BUILDINGS 18 B1
NEWCASTLE (County Down) 16 B3
NEWCASTLE (County Wicklow) 12 E2
NEWCASTLE WEST 4 C3
NEWCOMEN BRIDGE JUNCTION 12 B1
NEWCOURT 1 D2
NEWMARKET 4 E3
NEW MILLS 17 C4
NEWPORT 13 E1
NEW ROSS 6 D3
NEWRY BRIDGE STREET 16 B1
NEWRY DUBLIN BRIDGE 16 B1
NEWRY EDWARD STREET [BNT)] 16 B1
NEWRY EDWARD STREET [GNR(I)] 16 B1
NEWTON CUNNINGHAM 17 B5
  Originally named NEWTOWNCUNNINGHAM;
  also timetabled as NEWTON
NEWTOWNARDS 19 E3
NEWTOWNBUTLER 15 B1
NEWTOWNFORBES 14 F4
NEWTOWNSTEWART 18 E1
NOBBER 15 E4

O

OLDCASTLE 15 F2
OLDSTOWN 17 B4
OMAGH 18 F1
OMEATH 16 C1

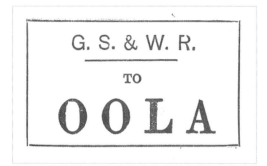

OOLA 5 B2
ORANMORE 9 C4
OUGHTERARD 9 B2

P

PALACE EAST 6 C4
PALLAS 5 B2
PARKMORE 19 B1
PASSAGE 2 A1
PATRICK'S WELL 4 B5
PEAKE 1 A4
PETTIGO 17 F4
PLUCK 17 B5
POMEROY 18 F3
PORTADOWN 18 G5
   Named PORTADOWN (CRAIGAVON WEST) 1970 –1971
PORTARLINGTON 11 D2
PORTHALL 18 C1
PORT HALT 17 E2
   Originally named PORT
PORTMARNOCK 12 B2

PORTRUSH 20 G4
PORTSTEWART 18 A4
PORTSTEWART [PT] 20 G4
POULAPHOUCA 11 D5
POYNTZPASS 15 A5
PROUDSTOWN PARK 15A G4
   Race traffic only

Q

QUEENSTOWN 2 A2
QUEENSTOWN JUNCTION 2 A2
QUILTY 9 G1

R

RACE COURSE PLATFORM 16A Inset F4
   Race traffic only
RAFFEEN 2 A1
   Also timetabled as RAFFEEN FOR SHANBALLY
RAHENY 12 B2
RANDALSTOWN 19 D1
RANDALSTOWN CAMP PLATFORM 19A D1
   Military halt
RAPHOE 17 C5
RASHENNY 20 G1
RATHCOOL 4 F4
RATHDRUM 12 F1
RATHDUFF 4 G5
RATHGAROGUE 6 C4
RATHKEALE 4 B4
RATHKENNY 19 C1
RATHMINES & RANELAGH 12 C1
RATHMORE 4 F2
RATHNEW FOR NEWRATH BRIDGE 12 E2
   Originally named NEWRATH
RATHPEACON 5 G1
   Goods only
RATHVILLY 11 F4
RECESS 8 A5
RECESS HOTEL PLATFORM 8A A5
REDHILLS 15 C1
RETREAT 19 B1
   Goods only
RICHHILL 18 G5
ROCHESTOWN 2 A1
ROCKCORRY 15 C3
ROSCOMMON 14 G2
ROSCREA 10 F4
ROSHARRY 14 D4
ROSS 9 B2
ROSSLARE HARBOUR 7 E1
ROSSLARE STRAND 7 E1
ROSSNOWLAGH 17 F2
ROSSTEMPLE 4 C5
ROSTREVOR 16 C1
RUAN 9 F3
RUSH & LUSK 12 A2
RUSHBROOKE 2 A2
   Originally named MONKSTOWN FERRY

S

ST ANNE'S 1 A5
SAINTFIELD 19 G3
ST JOHNSTON 18 C1
SALLINS 11 C4
SALLYBROOK 17 B5
SALTHILL 12 C2
SANDYCOVE 12 C2
   Originally named KINGSTOWN SANDYCOVE

SCARVA 15 A5

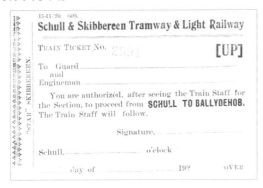

SCHULL 1 D1
SEAPOINT 12 C2
SHALLEE 10 G2
SHALLOGANS HALT 17A C2
SHANKILL 12 C2
  Also timetabled as SHANKILL (BRAY)
SHEAF 1 C4
SHILLELAGH 11 G5
SHOW GROUND HALT 2A Inset E3
  For show traffic only
SIDNEY PARADE 12 B1
SION MILLS 17 D5
SIXMILEBRIDGE 4 A4
SIXMILECROSS 18 F2
SKEAF 1 C4
SKERRIES 16 G2
SKIBBEREEN 1 D2
SLIGO 14 A1
SMITHBOROUGH 15 B2
SMYTH'S SIDING HALT 16A A1
SPA 3 D5
SPAMOUNT 17 D5
STAFFORDSTOWN 18 E5
STEWARTSTOWN 18 F4
STILLORGAN 12 C1
STRABANE 17 C5
STRAFFAN 11 C5
STRANOCUM 18 A5
STRANORLAR 17 D4
STREAMSTOWN 10 A5
STREET & RATHOWEN 14 G5
SUTTON & BALDOYLE 12 B2
  Originally named BALDOYLE & SUTTON
SWINFORD 13 D4
SYDENHAM 19 E3
  Originally named BALLYMISERT

T

TALLAGHT 12 C1
TALLOW ROAD 5 F3
TAMLAGHT HALT 18A C4
TANDERAGEE 18 G5
  Originally named MADDEN BRIDGE
TARA STREET 12 B1
  Originally named TARA STREET & GEORGE'S QUAY

TASSAGH 15 A4
TEMPLEMORE 10 G4
TEMPLEOGUE 12 C1
TEMPLEPATRICK 19 E2
TERENURE 12 C1
THE LAMB 11 C5
THOMASTOWN (County Kilkenny) 6 B2
THOMASTOWN (County Roscommon) 10 B3
THURLES 5 A4
TILLSBURN HALT 19 E3
TIMOLEAGUE 1 C4
TINAHELY 11 G5
TIPPERARY 5 C2
TIVOLI 2 A1
TOMKIN ROAD 14 C5
TOOBAN JUNCTION 18 B1
  Originally named JUNCTION;
    also known as LETTERKENNY JUNCTION
TOOME 18 D5
  Also timetabled as TOOME BRIDGE
TOWER BRIDGE 1 A5
TRALEE 3 E5

TRAMORE 6 F2
TREW & MOY 18 G4
TRILLICK 17 G5
TRIM 15 G4
TROOPER'S LANE 19 D3
TUAM 9 A4
TUBBER 9 E4
TUBBERCURRY 13 C5
TULLAMORE 10 C5
TULLOW 11 G4
TULLYMURRY 16 A3
TYNAN 15 A3
TYNAN & CALEDON 15 A3
  Originally named TYNAN, CALEDON & MIDDLETOWN

U-V

UPPERLANDS 18 C4
UPTON & INNISHANNON 1 B5
  Originally named BRINNY
VALENCIA HARBOUR 3 G2
  Also timetabled as VALENTIA HARBOUR
VERNERSBRIDGE 18 G4
  Originally named VERNER
VICTORIA 2 A1

VICTORIA BRIDGE [CVBT] 17 D5
VICTORIA BRIDGE [GNR(I)] 18 D1
VIRGINIA ROAD 15 F3

W

WARRENPOINT 16 C1
WATERFALL 1 A5
WATERFORD NORTH 6 E2
WATERFORD MANOR 6 E2
WELLINGTON BRIDGE 6 E4
WESTPORT 13 E1
WESTPORT QUAY 13 E1
WEXFORD 6 D5
WEXFORD SOUTH 6 D5
WHITEABBEY 19 E2
WHITEHEAD 19 D3
WHITEHOUSE 19 E2

WICKLOW 12 E2
WICKLOW MURROUGH 12A E2
WILKINSON 15 F4
WILLBROOK 9 F3
WOODBROOK 12A C2
   Golf course halt
WOODENBRIDGE JUNCTION 12 G1
   Originally named WOODENBRIDGE & SHILLELAGH
      JUNCTION
WOODLANDS 1 D1
WOODLAWN 10 B1
   Also timetabled as WOODLAWN FOR LOUGHREA
WORKHOUSE HALT 9A F2

Y

YORK ROAD 19 E2
   Originally named BELFAST YORK ROAD

YOUGHAL 2 A4

G. W. R.

IRELAND via FISHGUARD.

DAILY WEEK DAY SERVICE
Via

Fishguard & Rosslare.

To IRELAND.

	p.m.
London (Paddington) ....dep.	8 0
	a.m.
Fishguard Harbour ....arr.	1 40
	a.m.
Rosslare Harbour.......................arr.	5 20
Waterford .... ‚‚	7 0
Cork .... ‚‚	10 §0
	p.m.
Killarney .... ‚	12‡37
	a.m.
Dublin (Kingsbridge) .... ‚‚	10‡55

From IRELAND.

	p.m.
Dublin (Kingsbridge)...................dep.	6 15
Killarney .... ‚‚	4 12
Cork .... ‚‚	7 0
Waterford .... ‚‚	10 5
Rosslare Harbour.......................arr.	11 5
	a.m.
Fishguard Harbour ....dep.	3 25
London (Paddington) ....arr.	9 10

‡ Sundays excepted.   § On Sundays arrive Cork 12 0 noon.

Via

Fishguard & Waterford.

Direct Steamer.

To WATERFORD.

(Mondays, Wednesdays, & Fridays.)	p.m.
London (Paddington) ....dep.	5 0
Fishguard Harbour ....arr.	11 30
	a.m.
Waterford (Adelphi Wharf)....... .... arr. about	8 30

From WATERFORD.

(Tuesdays, Thursdays, & Saturdays.)	p.m.
Waterford (Adelphi Wharf) ....dep.	5 25
	a.m.
Fishguard Harbour ....dep.	3 25
London (Paddington) ....arr.	9 10

The above Services are subject to Alteration.

Via

Fishguard & Cork.

(City of Cork Steam Packet Company's Direct Steamer.)
Passengers are advised to book in advance.

To CORK.

(Tues., Thurs., and Sats.).	p.m.
London (Paddington) ....dep.	5 0
Fishguard Harbour ....arr.	11 30
	a.m.
Cork (Penrose Quay) .... arr. about	10 0

From CORK.

(Mons., Weds., and Fris.).	p.m.	
Cork (Penrose Quay) ....dep	6 0	
	a.m.	a.m.
Fishguard Harbour....................dep.	4 55	8 0
		p.m.
London (Paddington)..................arr.	10 57	2 30

Another advertisement from a 1922 *Bradshaw*, this time for the GWR's long ferry crossings to Ireland's southern ports.

GAZETTEER II – 2014 Stations

Map references of stations opened, reopened or renamed since 1 January, indexed alphabetically letter by letter. Replacement stations of the same name are not included (unless relocated to another line), nor are heritage railway stations sharing a common name.

A

ADAMSTOWN 11A B5
ADELAIDE 19A Inset B3
Renamed from ADELAIDE & WINDSOR
ANNACOTTY HALT 5A A1
On site of ANNACOTTY
(originally named GRANGE, closed 1863)
ANNAGH NO.2 HALT 9A G1
ANNALOUGHAN HALT 16A D1
ANNASCAUL 3A E3
Renamed from AUNASCAUL
ASHFIELD 19A G1
ATTYMON 9A C5
Renamed from ATTYMON JUNCTION

B

BALLINASARE 3A F3
Renamed from BALLINOSARE
BALLINASCARTY 1A C4
Renamed from BALLINASCARTHY [TCR]
BALLYGOWAN HALT 19A G1
BALLYHEATHER HALT 18A C1
BALLYNOE HALT 16A A3
Renamed from BALLYNOE
BANGOR WEST 19A E3
Originally named BANGOR WEST HALT
BARNES HALT 17A A4
Also known as No.8 GATES
BARN HALT 19A D3
Originally named TAYLOR'S CROSSING HALT
BAYSIDE 12A E5
BEACH HALT 17A A5
BEECHWOOD [Luas] 12A Inset F4
Renamed from RATHMINES & RANELAGH
BELFAST CENTRAL 19A Inset B4
BELLURGAN POINT HALT 16A D1
BLACKSTAFF HALT 15A C4
BLEACH GREEN HALT 19A E2
BOTANIC 19A Inset B4
BRAY (DALY) 12A D2
Renamed from BRAY
BRIGHT HALT 16A Inset F4
BROOKHILL HALT 19A F1
BROOMBRIDGE 12A Inset F3
BROOMHEDGE HALT 19A F1
BRUCKLESS HALT 17A E1
Renamed from BRUCKLESS
BUSHMILLS PLATFORM 20A G5
BUTTEVANT 4A E5
Renamed from BUTTEVANT & DONERAILE

C

CARNDOAGH HALT 20A G1
Also known as COLLIN HILL

CARRICHUE HALT 18A B2
Renamed from CARRICHUE
CARROWDUFF 10A B3
Renamed from THOMASTOWN (County Roscommon)
CASTLEKNOCK 12A Inset E3
CASTLETOWN HALT 15A F4
Previously open as CASTLETOWNPATRICK
CASTLETOWNROCHE & KILLAVULLEN 5A F1
Renamed from CASTLETOWNROCHE
CAVAN HALT 17A D4
CHERRY ORCHARD 12A Inset F3
CITY HOSPITAL 19A Inset B4
CLIPPERSTOWN 19A D3
Originally named CLIPPERSTOWN HALT
CLONDALKIN FONTHILL 12A Inset F3
Renamed from CLONDALKIN
CLONGRIFFEN 12A Inset E4
CLONTARF ROAD 12A Inset F4
CLOUNA HALT 9A F2
Also known as CLOONEY
COBH 2A Inset E5
Renamed from QUEENSTOWN
COLLOONEY SOUTH 14A B1
Renamed from COLLOONEY [GSWR]
CONEY ISLAND HALT 16A Inset G5
COOLMINE 12A Inset E2
COOLMORE HALT 17A F2
CORK (KENT) 2A Inset D3
Renamed from CORK GLANMIRE ROAD
CRAUGHWELL 9A C5
Renamed from CRAUGHWELL & LOUGHREA
CRAWFORDSBURN 19A E3
Originally named CRAWFORDSBURN HOSPITAL
CREEVYARGON HALT 19A G3
CROMORE 18A A4
Renamed from PORTSTEWART [NCC]
CROSSALANEY HALT 16A C1
CROSSBARRY 1A B5
Renamed from KINSALE JUNCTION
CULLION HALT 18A C1
Originally named CULLION

D

DAMHEAD HALT 19A F1
DERRAGHY 19A F2
Renamed from DERRIAGHY HALT
DHU VARREN 20A G4
DOCKLANDS 12A Inset F4
DOORIN ROAD HALT 17A E2
Renamed from DOORIN ROAD
DORRIAN'S BRIDGE HALT 17A F2
DOWNSHIRE 19A D3
Originally named BONEYBEFORE HALT
DRENNAN'S FARM 18A B2
World War II military halt

DROGHEDA MACBRIDE 16A F1
Renamed from DROGHEDA

DROMORE HALT 17A F2

DRUMADONALD 16A A2

DRUMBAR BRIDGE HALT 17A E3
Renamed from DRUMBAR HALT

DRUMCONDRA 12A Inset F4
Previously open 1901– c.1910

DRUMCULLION HALT 17A G5
World War II seaplane workers' halt

DRUMSOUGH 19A D1
Renamed from COOKSTOWN JUNCTION

DUBLIN (CONNOLLY) 12A Inset F4
Renamed from DUBLIN AMIENS STREET

DUBLIN (HEUSTON) 12A Inset F3
Renamed from DUBLIN KINGSBRIDGE

DUBLIN (PEARSE) 12A Inset F4
Renamed from DUBLIN WESTLAND ROAD

DUNDALK (CLARKE) 15A D5
Renamed from DUNDALK

DUNGLOE ROAD 17A B1
Renamed from DUNGLOE

DUN LAOGHAIRE (MALLIN) 12A Inset G5
Renamed from KINGSTOWN, then DUN LAOGHAIRE

E

EDEN HALT 19A D3

ELATAGH HALT 17A C3

EXHIBITION HALT 2A Inset E3 1932
Temporary halt

F

FAIRVIEW DEPOT STAFF HALT 12A Inset F4

FINAGHY 19A F2
Renamed from FINAGHY HALT

FITZGERALD PLATFORM 4A F1
For sports stadium traffic only

FRASER STREET HALT 19A Inset B4

FRIARY HALT 17A F2

G

GALWAY (CEANNT) 9A C3
Renamed from GALWAY

GLASSAGH HALT 17A C3

GLASS MOSS ROAD HALT 19A F3
Used only for TT Car Race traffic 1928 –1936

GLENAGALT 3A E4
Renamed from GLOUNAGALT BRIDGE;
also known as GLENAGALT BRIDGE

GLENANNE 15A A5
Renamed from LOUGHGILLY

GLENMORE 6A D3
Renamed from GLENMORE & AYLWARDSTOWN

GLOUNTHAUNE 2A Inset D5
Renamed from QUEENSTOWN JUNCTION

GOODYEAR 18A G5

GORTALOUGHAN HALT 17A G5

GRACEHILL HALT 18A A5
Renamed from GRACEHILL

GRAND CANAL DOCK 12A Inset F4

GYLES QUAY HALT 16A D1

H

HANSFIELD 11A B5

HANRAHAN'S BRIDGE 9A F2
Also known as MOY BRIDGE

HARMONSTOWN 12A Inset E4

HENRYVILLE HALT 19A Inset B5
Used only for TT Car Race traffic 1928 –1936

HILDEN 19A F2
Renamed from HILDEN HALT

HOSPITAL HALT 17A E3

HOWTH JUNCTION & DONAGHMEDE
                              12A Inset E5
Renamed from HOWTH JUNCTION

I

INCH ABBEY 16A Inset F4

K

KELLYBRIDGE HALT 15A D5

KILBARRACK 12A Inset E4

KILCOOLE 12A D2
Renamed from KILCOOL

KILGOBBIN HALT 4A B5

KILKENNY (MACDONAGH) 6A A2
Renamed from KILKENNY

KILLESTER 12A Inset F4

KILMAKERRILL 14A A3

KILMOKEA HALT 6A E3
Temporary halt for power station construction workers 1966
                                      –1968

KILROOT HALT 19A D3
Renamed from KILROOT

KING'S MOSS HALT 19A D2

KINGSTOWN PIER, DUN LAOGHAIRE
                              12A Inset G5
Renamed from KINGSTOWN CARLISLE PIER

KNOCKBUE HALT 1A C2
Renamed from KNUCKBUE

KNOCKMORE 19A F2

KNOCKMORE JUNCTION HALT 19A F2

L

LAMBERTON'S HALT 17A A5

LARNE TOWN 19A C3
Replaced LARNE [std gauge]

LAYTOWN 16A F1
Renamed from LAYTOWN & BETTYSTOWN

LEGATIRIFF HALT 19A F1

LEIXLIP (CONFEY) 11A B5

LEIXLIP (LOUISA BRIDGE) 11A B5
Renamed from LEIXLIP [MGWR]

LIFFORD HALT 9A F3

LIMERICK (COLBERT) 4A A5
Renamed from LIMERICK

LISAHALLY 18A B1
World War II military halt

LISFANNON GOLF LINKS 17A A5
Renamed from GOLF HALT or PLATFORM

STATION NAMES

Whilst every effort has been made to ensure that the station names in this Railway Atlas are correct, it should be remembered that in some cases a choice has had to be made from a number of contenders:

– the name generally used by the railway company
– the name that appeared in (non-company) timetables
– the name used by other railway companies for through ticketing purposes
– and even the name on the station signs

For example, establishing just how 'official' the suffix 'FOR SUCH-AND-SUCH A PLACE' was has been fraught with difficulty. Also, when a station was demoted to an unstaffed halt – as many were, as a cost-cutting exercise – was its new official status acknowledged by an official change of name? And if so, did anyone bother to alter the nameboard(s)? Many putative changes of name of this sort have therefore been ignored

For historical and commercial reasons, a place served by two companies might well have had two stations of exactly the same name – especially where a standard gauge and a narrow gauge railway served the same town. With increasing rationalisation of the network, any such standard gauge/narrow gauge anomalies tended to quickly disappear; likewise, a station soon lost its 'JUNCTION' suffix when the branch leading from it was closed. In addition, transliterations of Irish place-names have sometimes changed over the years – occasionally the name of a station would be spelled differently from the name of the place it served! In the case of modern station names, the form used on the appropriate official website has been adopted.

Finally, in the interests of historical accuracy any verifiable corrections to the station names used – or indeed any other aspect of this Atlas – will be welcomed by the compilers.

The end of the line: the sorry-looking remains of the turntable at Galway station, a rusting relic of a vanished age.   *Harry Maeers*